DIRECT CONTACT

CAMERALESS PHOTOGRAPHY NOW

LAUREN RICHMAN

Sidney and Lois Eskenazi Museum of Art
INDIANA UNIVERSITY

Published to accompany the exhibition *Direct Contact: Cameraless Photography Now*, organized by the Sidney and Lois Eskenazi Museum of Art, Indiana University, Bloomington.

Generous support for this publication was provided in part by Martha and David Moore, Patrick and Jane Martin, and Jim and Joyce Grandorf.

Sidney and Lois Eskenazi Museum of Art
Indiana University
1133 East Seventh Street
Bloomington, Indiana 47405-7509
artmuseum.indiana.edu

Designed and typeset by Jessie Waymire
Edited by Mariah R. Keller
Set in Apparat type, printed on
100# Anthem Plus Satin Text white (interior)
and 10pt Kallima/Spectro C1S white (cover)
Printed by Printing Partners of
Indianapolis, Indiana

Library of Congress Cataloguing-in-Publication Data

Names: Richman, Lauren, editor. | Sidney and Lois Eskenazi Museum of Art, host institution.
Title: Direct contact : cameraless photography now / Lauren Richman.
Description: Bloomington, Indiana : Sidney and Lois Eskenazi Museum of Art, Indiana University, Bloomington, [2023] | "Published to accompany the exhibition Direct Contact: Cameraless Photography Now, organized by the Sidney and Lois Eskenazi Museum of Art, Indiana University, Bloomington"--Page facing title page. | Includes bibliographical references. | Summary: "Focusing on the material and tactile properties of the medium, Direct Contact: Cameraless Photography Now is the first contemporary survey to examine cameraless photography across generations, cultures, and ideologies. Referred to as photograms or contact prints, cameraless photographs are made using analogue photography's foundational elements: light, chemistry, and light-sensitive surfaces. Presenting recent work by more than 40 artists-including Yto Barrada, InŽaki Bonillas, Ellen Carey, Hernease Davis, Sheree Hovsepian, Roberto Huarcaya, Kei Ito, Dakota Mace, Fabiola Menchelli, Lisa Oppenheim, Daisuke Yokota, among many others-Direct Contact highlights many emerging global artists and features primarily women-identifying artists. Unfolding across five sections-Age, Scale, Form, Texture, and Value-Direct Contact positions cameraless photography as both an intellectual cornerstone in the medium's history and an enduring and important force within contemporary art"-- Provided by publisher.

Identifiers: LCCN 2022047110 | ISBN 9798218079901 (paperback)
Subjects: LCSH: Photography, Abstract--Exhibitions. | Photograms--Exhibitions. | Contact printing--Exhibitions. | Installations (Art)--Exhibitions.
Classification: LCC TR645.B576 S533 2023 | DDC 770.74--dc23/eng/20221207
LC record available at https://lccn.loc.gov/2022047110

Cover: Daisuke Yokota, detail of *Untitled* (p. 39)

Page 4: Mariah Robertson, detail of *150 151* (p. 36)

Page 26: Daisuke Yokota, detail of *Untitled* (p. 39)

Page 28: Anna Katharina Scheidegger, detail of *Untitled* (p. 37)

Page 40: Justine Varga, detail of *Masseuse* (p. 51)

Page 52: Elizabeth M. Claffey, detail of *Archived Attempts 1* (p. 56)

Page 64: Marta Djourina, detail of *Untitled* (p. 69)

Page 76: Farrah Karapetian, detail of *Distress Day 1* (p. 83)

Page 86: Hernease Davis, detail of *Bare with Me, Foundation, 17* (page 58)

Page 99: Photo by Shanti Knight

CONTENTS

DIRECTOR'S FOREWORD

When Henry Holmes Smith arrived in Bloomington, Indiana, in 1947 to create the fine art photography program at Indiana University (IU), he was probably aware that he was breaking new ground. Following the early efforts of Clarence White to establish a fine arts photography teaching program at Ohio University in the first half of the twentieth century, Smith was among the early pioneers in establishing photography as an academic fine arts discipline in the United States. Smith went on to become a renowned teacher of photography, mentoring a number of important students, including Jerry Uelsmann, Jack Welpott, and Betty Hahn, to name a few.

In some ways, the work of Smith's students became better known than that of their teacher. Perhaps he did not prioritize the commercial side of his practice or he put so much effort into teaching. The fact that the market for photography was not yet established may also be a factor. Whatever the reason, the lion's share of Smith's artistic output, numbering several thousand prints, made their way into the collections of IU's Eskenazi Museum of Art, where they have resided quietly for several decades.

Thanks to the efforts of Dr. Lauren Richman, we now know a great deal more about Smith and his practice, which focused on the production of photographic images without the use of a camera. These colorful, painterly prints are the result of decades of experimentation and trial and error. Through his technique of dripping Karo® corn syrup onto a glass plate, he seems almost to have translated Jackson Pollock's famous drip technique into the field of photography. We trust that Dr. Richman's research and that of future Smith scholars will find their way into the world and will allow Smith's efforts to be appreciated by a wider audience.

Given IU's unique history in the field of cameraless photography through the pioneering efforts of Smith, I asked Dr. Richman to investigate the field of contemporary cameraless photography to see what, if anything, was happening today in this branch of photography. She discovered that cameraless photography is very much alive and well and being practiced all over the world by a diverse range of talented artists. *Direct Contact* includes the work of photographers from approximately twenty countries, including Australia, South Africa, Bulgaria, and Israel, and features primarily women-identifying artists. I want to take this opportunity to thank and acknowledge Dr. Richman's good work in providing this fascinating and insightful overview of contemporary cameraless photography.

As with any exhibition and catalogue, this project has been a team effort. Dr. Richman will name many colleagues in her acknowledgments, but I want to particularly thank the Henry R. Luce Foundation for making Dr. Richman's tenure at IU possible. In addition, I am grateful to Martha and David Moore for their enthusiastic and generous support of the photography program at the Eskenazi Museum of Art. Thanks also to Jim and Joyce Grandorf for their help in making the book a reality. And finally, I would like to thank Patrick and Jane Martin for their support of the museum's publication program and for their support of this catalogue, which we are sharing, free of charge, with our museum's *Schema* subscribers.

One of our primary institutional goals is to connect the art of the past with the art of the present, and this exhibition does just that. We have acquired a number of cameraless works in advance of the exhibition, demonstrating our continued commitment to diversifying the museum's collection with the addition of contemporary art. Although most of the artists represented in the exhibition had probably never heard of Henry Holmes Smith, their work enables us to look back with greater appreciation to the work of previous generations and demonstrate that great ideas continue to spread and flourish without regard for space and time limitations. This connectivity of ideas is what makes our field so great, and I invite you to discover this for yourself in the art of *Direct Contact*.

David A. Brenneman
Wilma E. Kelley Director, Eskenazi Museum of Art

AUTHOR'S ACKNOWLEDGMENTS

This project is the result of many thought-provoking conversations and studio visits, with people near and far. I extend my thanks to the participating artists and their galleries, whose engaging work marks both the beginning and end of this rewarding endeavor.

My work on this project was made possible through the generosity of the Henry Luce Foundation, which provided grant funding to support my research on the IU Eskenazi Museum of Art's Henry Holmes Smith Archive.

I am also grateful to my colleagues at the Eskenazi Museum, especially David A. Brenneman, Wilma E. Kelley Director, for his persistent belief in my work and Director of Curatorial Affairs Danielle Johnson, for her commitment to my vision and constant support. My gratitude extends to Director of Creative Services and Editor Mariah Keller for her management of this publication; Registrar Emma Fulce, for her advice, steadfast positivity, and friendship; and Graphic Design Manager Jessie Waymire, for designing a stunning catalogue. To Chief Preparator Pete Nelson and Senior Preparator Max Shaw, thank you for humoring my persistent inquiries and your dedication to the exhibition layout. Much appreciation extends to former Henry Holmes Smith Archive Registrar's Assistant Gabby Krieble for her contributions to the glossary; Works on Paper Preparator Janelle Grimmer; Associate Registrar Heather Hales; and all of our skilled Art Handlers. Many thanks to our outstanding Education, Development, Conservation, and Security and Guest Services teams; and my fellow curators, including Lucienne M. Glaubinger Curator of Works on Paper Nanette Esseck Brewer, for their curiosity and driving questions.

The Eskenazi Museum is lucky to have a National Advisory Board comprised of donors who are deeply engaged in our work. I extend sincere thanks to longtime champions of photography, Martha and David Moore, and stalwart advocates of museum publications, Patrick and Jane Martin, and Jim and Joyce Grandorf, for their generous support of the exhibition catalogue.

As I connected with artists outside of Bloomington, I was reminded of the magnificent reach and influence of IU colleagues, including James Nakagawa, Liz Claffey, David Ondrik, Dr. Faye Gleisser, and Dr. Vivek Vellanki, whose energy, excitement, and feedback is much appreciated. Special thanks to artist Emeka Okérèké for engaging in meaningful conversations about the present and future of photography during his time at IU.

To my parents, Joel and Francine Richman, few words can encompass what your support means to me. Thank you for your sincere curiosity in my work, creative solutions, and encouragement. Special thanks to my friends, Cameron, Emma, Rachel, Kelly, Galina, Julie, and Kelli for their inquisitive minds and restorative laughs. Finally, to Christopher Goodman (and Frankie): your unwavering love and conviction in my abilities is unmatched and felt daily. Thank you for being the best kind of partner. I cannot wait to see what is next.

Fig. 1. Henry Holmes Smith (American, 1909–1986). *Untitled*, 1973. Dye transfer print, image: 13 x 10 1/16 in. (33 x 25.6 cm); sheet: 13 15/16 x 11 1/16 in. (35.4 x 28.1 cm). Eskenazi Museum of Art, Indiana University, 79.200.XV.26

DIRECT CONTACT
CAMERALESS PHOTOGRAPHY NOW

How does one experience a photograph that appears "unphotographic"?[1]

An assemblage of deep blue-green shards rises from the center of the composition, encompassed by a swelling fuchsia landscape (fig. 1). Evocative of a mountain summit, they pierce a billowing, myrtle green cloud that appears to repel from the vermilion base layer. A faint, lunar circle hangs in delicate suspension in the center. This 1973 photograph by Henry Holmes Smith (American, 1909–1986) displays a multitude of colors and forms that meld together just as readily as they stand apart. The unexpected simultaneity of the work's representational and non-representational forms compels second and third looks, while encouraging readings to shift and evolve over time. Perhaps the most pressing questions are: what is this and how was it made?

Since its conception in the nineteenth century, there has been a driving preoccupation with defining photography. More often than not the consensus is a gray area between binaries: presence and absence, light and shadow, positive and negative, living and dead, representational and non-representational. The subtext of this desire might be best described as a sense of anxiety related to the medium of photography: a need to understand what it is and how it is made. Unlike many other visual media, photography's alchemical properties intimate a sense of "magic." It is somehow both a mechanical technology that records a physical transformation and one that happens beyond our sight. This produces a multitude of responses, including discomfort and confusion, but also a kind of concession to photography's inherent enigma.

Bolstering this history and process is the camera apparatus. Photographs made with cameras hold associations with objectivity, reality, and truth—"an eye onto the world." However, the camera, like the photographer, possesses a powerful capacity to code, construct, and signal. Every photograph—no matter how evidential-seeming—can produce infinite realities and discourses.[2] What happens, then, when the camera is removed from the equation?

As Smith's work demonstrates, viewers are confronted with a much less familiar object. However, cameraless photographs uniquely necessitate direct contact between the object or element being recorded and the chemically treated, light-sensitive surface. Also referred to as contact prints, they constitute the earliest form of the photographic object. Despite this, the history of cameraless photography is much less visible than its counterpart. For one, it is nonlinear in its global development and it defies the so-called logic of reproducibility that is central to the otherwise mechanical medium. Added to this obstacle are the relative ambiguities of photographic abstraction and, in some cases, the use of color that does not correspond with everyday life. The result is a branch of photography disoriented from its own history and even relegated to its margins as a technical preparatory exercise that might prefigure the operation of a camera.

The exhibition *Direct Contact: Cameraless Photography Now* instead positions the cameraless object as both an intellectual cornerstone of the history of photography and an enduring and important force within contemporary art. Featuring the work of forty-two artists, it is the first survey to focus on contemporary explorations of cameraless photography across generations, cultures, and ideologies, while highlighting many emerging artists and featuring primarily women-identifying artists. Past exhibitions on such work have not adequately represented or examined the global nature of the practice. Unfolding across five sections—age, scale, form, texture, and value—*Direct Contact* addresses a continuing artistic desire to confront the unplanned and imperfect. In doing so, the exhibition foregrounds discussions of photography's materiality and encourages slow looking.

At the center of the exhibition is also the concept of touch, an especially meaningful notion today. Despite being daily operators of photography and images, screens have become its most common vessel. We rarely use our hands to fold, crop, and manipulate photographs, or feel their weight, texture, and surface finish. The images on our screens do not yellow or age by accruing bent corners and creased edges, nor do they display handwritten dates, descriptions, or personal anecdotes on the reverse side. Photographs almost exist out of time now. Although digital photography has given us mobility, endless distribution, and instantaneous feedback, we pay less attention to technical or material processes. As such, *Direct Contact* places the artist's material intervention at the locus of the discussion, supported by cultural, theoretical, political, and personal narratives.

If we consider Smith as a point of departure, *Direct Contact* holds relevance to the Sidney and Lois Eskenazi Museum of Art, as well as the Indiana University (IU) and Bloomington communities. Smith—who was invited by László Moholy-Nagy (Hungarian, 1895–1946) to teach the first light workshop at the New Bauhaus—brought a radically different attitude on the medium's role within the broader visual arts when he was hired in 1947 as IU's first professor of photography. Since his hire, both the Eskenazi Museum and the IU Eskenazi School of Art, Architecture + Design have embraced the acquisition and teaching of experimental photography. As a continuation of these efforts, this exhibition also highlights several new acquisitions made by the museum in 2021 and 2022 that support its continued institutional mission to cultivate more progressive and equitable collecting and exhibition practices.

Begin

Photography's origin story commonly begins with an 1827 heliograph taken by scientist and inventor Joseph Nicéphore Niépce (French, 1765–1833) (fig. 2). Heliography, as defined by Niépce, involved coating a pewter plate with the chemical solution Bitumen of Judea, inserting the plate into a handheld camera obscura, and exposing it to natural sunlight for about eight hours.[3] This process resulted in the earliest known permanent positive image made using a camera apparatus. Taken from his second-story window in Saint-Loup-de-Varennes, France, viewers might identify a traditional linear perspective: building rooftops and treetops situated against a clear horizon line.

Mythologized (and later, cleverly marketed) as "the first photograph," this object embodies a dominant history of photography that contributes to an unfair obfuscation of its vital counter-history: cameraless photography.[4] Such objects can be traced back as far as 1717, when physician and polymath Johann Heinrich Schulze (German, 1687–1744) accidentally discovered

Fig. 2. Joseph Nicéphore Niépce (French, 1765–1833). *Untitled 'point de vue,'* 1827. Heliograph on pewter, 16.7 x 20.3 x .15 cm. Gernsheim Collection, purchase, 964:0000:0001

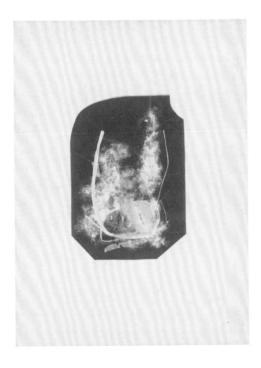

Fig. 3. Christian Schad (German, 1894–1982). *Schadograph,* 1919. Gelatin silver chloride photogram, 3 ¼ x 2 ¼ in. (8.3 x 5.8 cm). Art Institute of Chicago, 2014.1180

the sensitivity of silver salts to light. Although Schulze was unable to fix his images, it is this interaction between light, chemistry, and surface that laid the groundwork for photographic experimentation. Schulze's name, however, is not often associated with the medium's historical beginnings.

The challenges central to elevating this counter-history are manifold. First, the countless players who figure into its global historical narrative make it difficult to define and nearly impossible to pinpoint anything as palpable as "the first cameraless photograph." Second, cameraless photographs have long been considered anticipatory experiments that lead to images made with cameras. Finally, with the emergence of commercial photography in the mid-nineteenth century, came the overshadowing demand for portraits and landscapes. Above all, photography was long considered a scientific and journalistic tool rather than an artistic medium—many major art museums did not begin exhibiting or collecting photography until the 1960s and 1970s. In this sense, historical figures like Smith pursued a nontraditional path marked with obstacles. His work follows crucial experimental contributions from artists during the interwar period, including Christian Schad (German, 1894–1982), László Moholy-Nagy (Hungarian, 1895–1946), Man Ray (American, 1890–1976) and Lee Miller (American, 1907–1977).

Placing Schad's 1919 *Schadograph* (fig. 3) in dialogue with Niépce's camera object divulges much about these parallel histories.[5] Schad selected rubbish and discarded materials, laid them onto light-sensitive paper, then covered the composition with a glass plate, exposing it to light from his basement apartment's windowsill. After exposure and fixing, he cut the image out with asymmetrical edges to "free [it] from the convention of the square."[6] In the context of Zurich's Dada movement—founded in reaction to the horrors and chaos of the First World War—Schad's arrangements read decidedly subversive in tone and appearance. Consider Schad's cut-up basement detritus in comparison to Niépce's serene second-floor landscape. In this sense, cameraless photography's reinvigoration was built upon an assault of its very tradition. Perhaps its fate was doomed from the start.

Here

Smith's earliest experiments with cameraless photography began in the 1930s with black-and-white photograms and evolved into other techniques and alternative processes. Creating a cameraless photograph was also Smith's first assignment in his 1937 light workshop for students of the New Bauhaus. By establishing the photogram as the foundation of his pedagogy, Smith's classroom became a welcome space for more experimental techniques and provocative viewpoints on the meaning, interpretation, and intellectual status of photography as an artistic medium.

In 1947, Smith's student Clyde "Red" Hare brought a bottle of Karo© corn syrup into the classroom. Although Hare's objective has been lost to history, Smith was drawn to the material's experimental viability.[7] He soon developed a unique method for creating cameraless photographs, further demonstrating to students that the photographic device demanded reconsideration. After laying out a sheet of light-sensitive paper in the dark, he poured corn syrup and water onto a glass or Plexi sheet. Raising it vertically to allow the mixture to move, Smith used a foot pedal to activate a 100-watt theater spotlight and create an exposure. Process-oriented, physically involved, and requiring the release of a certain degree of control, Smith's refraction prints took on the qualities of both photographs and paintings. *Grotesque* (fig. 4) features an aqueous blob in the center of the composition that almost bulges from the surface of the paper. Disordered drips and dribbles extending from the central form demonstrate crucial principles of improvisation and chance.

By the 1970s, Smith was adding vibrant color dyes to his refraction prints using dye transfer: a mechanical color printing process that he had been experimenting with as early as 1936.[8] By layering several matrices and purposely printing out of register, he further blurred the boundaries between figuration and abstraction. Smith's preoccupation with color likewise grew from a desire to belie anticipated or predetermined outcomes associated with photographic representation. By eschewing "naturalistic" or "lifelike" applications, he believed "synthetic color" could both access and express intimate emotions. Prolific in their color variations, Smith's photographs usher viewers into mind-bending psychedelic vistas. As Smith's student Betty Hahn wrote in 1973, "There is the feeling of standing in the presence of colors never seen before . . . the colors inherent in each image seemed to have been orchestrated, made to resound and flow in chromatic harmony."[9]

Death of Punch (fig. 5) similarly gestures toward a hallucinatory vision: yellow fragments spread like confetti across a black ground. Buttressed by red and green borders, the two-dimensional silhouettes appear to transmute into three-dimensional forms. According to Smith, the original print was made in December 1959 after one of his sons accidentally broke a glass Christmas ornament. Recognizing its poetic value, Smith immediately placed the shards atop matrix film to create an exposure. Likely referencing the *Punch and Judy* puppet show—in which the character of Punch is a murderous trickster who fools everyone he encounters, even outsmarting the devil himself—Smith's title suggests that the image addresses the character's

Fig. 4. Henry Holmes Smith (American, 1909–1986). *Grotesque*, 1950. Dye transfer print, 10 ⅞ x 8 ¹⁵⁄₁₆ in. (27.6 x 22.7 cm). Henry Holmes Smith Archive, Eskenazi Museum of Art, Indiana University, 73.471

Fig. 5. Henry Holmes Smith (American, 1909–1986). *Death of Punch*, 1975. Dye transfer print, image: 13 ¹⁵⁄₁₆ x 10 ³⁄₁₆ in. (35.4 x 25.9 cm); sheet: 13 ¹⁵⁄₁₆ x 11 ¹⁄₁₆ in. (35.4 x 28.1 cm). Henry Holmes Smith Archive, Eskenazi Museum of Art, Indiana University, 79.200.XV.15

ultimate demise. Through the lens of Smith's philosophies on photography, we might consider Punch as a substitute for the camera apparatus: a deceptive device responsible for misleading its makers and viewers to believe it is an agent of truth. Illustrated shattered and strewn across the ground, *Death of Punch* could be interpreted as an allegory for the death of representation. The direct contact between glass shard and matrix film—or, touch, as it is analogously addressed throughout this exhibition—generates a unique relationship between object, maker, and viewer, in which the photograph, often considered a container for something else, evolves into a container for itself.

Now

Returning to the present, *Direct Contact* brings together an exceptionally diverse body of work by artists who are invested in broad reconsiderations of representation. Smith's eschewal of "camera representation" was primarily an attack on realism, naturalistic color, and the concept that photography can and should tell the viewer exactly at what they are looking. In the contemporary context—built upon a lineage of which Smith is certainly part—debates on representation have extended to address postmodernism and its death, postcolonialism, queer theory, cyborg theory, and so on. The photographic medium has also achieved a higher and more stable rank within the hierarchy of the visual arts. On the surface, it appears that photography has also shed its historic link to purist thinking (sharp focus, high contrast, and rich tones and details, with no room for error or imperfections); however, the old guard lingers still. Although most of the artists included in the exhibition connect this issue directly to photography, many of them do not exclusively identify as photographers, and some have not undergone professional training or education in photography. As a whole, the conventional rules and expectations for the medium are no longer the sole, guiding principles for production or interpretation. It is through a selection of these material elements—age, scale, form, texture, and value—that the exhibition and discussion are organized.

AGE

Korean-Canadian artist Laurie Kang frequently works with unfixed photographic materials. Her objects fade, darken, warp, and transform the longer they are exposed to light. Unless she performs some sort of concrete intervention, Kang does not possess much control over what or how this process unfolds. This is also true for Japanese artist Daisuke Yokota, whose absorbing compositions are created using expired, but unused, large-format color film. Yokota's obsessive and repetitive process involves boiled water, fire, and "incorrect" chemicals that enact violence onto the film's surface. Although there is a certain measure of control, much is left to the material. Similarly, working with the sun as his primary agent, American artist Chris Duncan has grown quite comfortable with anticipating the unknown. Over extensive durations, Duncan leaves his textile-based objects undisturbed to transform under the sun's rays. When the property of permanence is removed, or material changes are extricated from the artist's control, time and nature assume conductorship.

In fact, the notion of nature's autonomous role in image formation was a significant component in the earliest findings of the photography pioneer William Henry Fox Talbot (British, 1800–1877). Presented to the Royal Society of Great Britain under the title "Some Account of the Art of Photogenic Drawing, or the Process by Which Natural Drawing Objects May Be Made to Delineate Themselves Without the Aid of the Artist's Pencil," Talbot's theory relied heavily upon the discovery that with this new technology nature could speak for itself. Unfettered by the artist's subjective hand, "self-delineation" contributed to photography's novelty and use-value, isolating it from other visual media of the time.

For Kang, an openness to change and intuitive decision-making is what her work requires. *Guts* (pp. 32–33) joins ribboned scraps of gauze and mesh fruit bags, food items like dried seaweed or the peels of mandarin oranges (familiar to Kang from frequent childhood visits to Korean and Asian supermarkets), and what appear to be a frying pan, kitchen sieve, and perforated disc. Arranged over light-sensitive paper, Kang exposes the individual photograms to sunlight, never stopping the development process nor fixing the works. Kang calls this "tanning," a term she coined and one that extends to her largescale, rolls of film that often hang from lighting tracks like animal hides (fig. 6). The threshold on which these unstable images hinge, between the past tense and an ongoing future tense, speaks to Kang's interests in liminality, hybridity, and porosity. In this sense, materials and their inherent "mis-use" are critical to Kang's broader explorations of her own hybrid cultural identity, ancestral inheritance, and the cyclical looping of it all.

Rather than allowing new materials to remain unfixed, Yokota purposely integrates unused large-format film that has already expired. An implication that the material is no longer "good," expiry defines an even greater relinquishment of material control. Although his process is improvisational, it also embraces a rigid structure. Yokota follows a similar choreography each time he creates new prints: after layering several variable sized sheets of expired film, he launches into an unorthodox development process. The artist scorches the film with boiling water, thus melting the delicate surface layers of emulsion and causing the silver to oxidize. Effectively

Fig. 6. Laurie Kang (Korean-Canadian, b. 1985). *Molt* (installation view, Horizon Art Foundation, Los Angeles, USA), 2022. Tanned and unfixed film (continually sensitive), spherical magnets, and cast aluminum fungus, variable installation dimensions. Courtesy of the artist

halting the development process, the damaged film can no longer be productive. The results are a hallucinatory, almost frenetic display of color, organic form, and meticulous record of texture. Although Yokota's ongoing series of color photographs shares some formal qualities with Smith's work, Yokota's work is a distillation of time, lacking any reference (neither motif, nor title) to anything at all. Curiously, in an *Untitled* (p. 39) work from the Eskenazi Museum's collection, Yokota's fingerprint is visible at a gigantic scale. It is a surprising visualization of human intervention in an otherwise completely abstract composition.

Duncan relies heavily upon nature, specifically the sun, to produce minimal compositions that pivot between photography, painting, and sculpture. He first chooses various manufactured color textiles to hang or drape across his bedroom windows, studio skylights, and open rooftops, or wrap and pin around ordinary objects like bricks, amplifiers, and drums. Without treating the fabric with light-sensitive chemistry, Duncan allows each textile to absorb sunlight—and, if arranged outside, incur damage from wind, rain, or snow—and oxidize over hyper-extended periods of time. Exposures take place over the course of six months to a year, testing the limits of the sun's effects, but also the patience of the artist. Can we consider this process photographic? Think about the last time you were out in the sun for so long that its rays left an impression on your skin—sunburn, tan lines, or suntan. There is something poetic about our own sensitivity and vulnerability to light. In dialogue with Kang's "mis-use" of materials, Duncan breaks every rule of photographic conservation by forcing the fabric's vulnerabilities to be seen and made permanent. Exemplified in *Orange Skylight (6 Month Exposure)* (p. 30), he adds supplementary materials to the object: saturated acrylic paint, thread, or both. In doing so, Duncan offers a tangible vestige of the artist's hand and an inversion of the work's rapport with architecture. What was at first a direct response to the architecture of a space or object, is now contained and made interior. Duncan's method forces us to contemplate the fundamental role that time plays in our contemporary experience. Slowing down does not come easy for a society habituated to the endless (doom) scroll, looped video content, or persistent expectations of immediacy from social media, our employers, and even our peers. To wait is to protest this status quo.

SCALE

The relationship between photography and scale is fraught: with a contact print, the scale cannot be altered; with a lens-based negative, the subject is miniaturized only later to be enlarged during printing.[10] Historically, the scale of a photographic print could not be altered. Photographs functioned as private, handheld objects or those meant to rest on a table or live within an album. As photography crossed into the realm of the visual arts through public exhibition, and later gained relevance on the commercial market in the 1970s and 1980s, drastically enlarged photographs became more common. These immersive tableaux are exemplified in the work of artists such as Jeff Wall and those associated with the Düsseldorf School (Thomas Struth, Candida Höfer, or Andreas Gursky).[11] This caused a major shift in viewing experience and positioned photography closer to history painting and minimalist sculpture by diverting attention away from its mechanical birthmark, reducing the volume of works shown in a single exhibition, and demanding more space, deeper consideration, and increased legitimacy.

In addition, the physical demands of *making*, especially using analogue materials, have always been an important facet of resurgent interest in cameraless techniques. This is especially true of large-format works, which require more physical space for chemical processing. With increasingly limited access to wet laboratory darkrooms each year, artists committed to analogue processes either modify their practices or devise their own darkroom spaces. For Peruvian artist Roberto Huarcaya this is in a makeshift darkroom tent in the middle of the Amazon rainforest; for American artist Joy Episalla it is in a small studio darkroom in which she uses garbage

Fig. 7. Roberto Huarcaya (Peruvian, b. 1959). *Amazograms* (installation view, Casa Rímac, Lima, Peru, 2014), 2014. Three gelatin silver photograms, 98 ft 5 in. x 3 ft 6 ½ in. (30 x 1.08 m). Courtesy of the artist

bags as developing trays. In both cases, scale has a profound impact on process, experience, and interpretation.

Since 2014, Huarcaya's focus has been on his immediate environment: Peru and its connections to expansive ecosystems like the Amazon rainforest and South Pacific Ocean.[12] After deeming his early lens-based attempts to record these living, constantly evolving environs a failure, he turned to the photogram. Huarcaya believes that the photogram has the ability not only to create a direct impression but also to provide a conceptual device for mediation between the artist and the landscape; he calls these works "frames." For his first series, *Amazograms*, Huarcaya threaded three 100-foot rolls of light-sensitive photo paper through dense foliage, trees, and mud (fig. 7). The works—which were completely vulnerable to the wet air of the tropical rainforest—were exposed to moonlight as the dominant light source, with some instances of handheld flash devices. Developed with river water over the course of nearly six hours, the enveloping prints describe the seemingly infinite sprawl of the landscape and chaos of the photographic process. For his most recent project, *Océanos* (pp.46–47), Huarcaya followed a similar practice: choreographing several people (colleagues, friends, and family) as they hauled a 200-foot roll of photo paper into the turbulent waters of the Pacific Ocean. Divided into three acts—the wave's approach, impact, and retreat—the process revealed that the ocean required different conditions and tools. The sea's constant state of flux also necessitated shorter exposure times and a more delicate fiber paper to record the subtleties of its intensity. If the *Amazograms* undulate through exhibition spaces with a rush of movement, the *Océanos* flood viewers with their panoramic magnitude and radiant, organic patterns.

Whereas Huarcaya attempts to distill the monolithic into a single "frame," Episalla coalesces photography's "aliveness" with distinct architectural spaces.[13] During a studio visit with Episalla, they retold the story of their first serious pivot toward the photogram. In 2013, Episalla planned a trip to Normandy both to visit a friend and the site where their beloved great uncle is buried. It was also during this visit that Episalla began experimenting with photograms using saltwater at the sea's edge. Under moonlight, they became reacquainted with the ocean's sprawl and vigor, while recognizing its relative kinship with photography. Both the sea and the analogue development process retain a persistent sense of motion and instability, fighting against any single, stationary condition. Episalla began to expand their thinking and after years of testing, they developed a process and set of materials that functioned best. Over the course of one week, Episalla produced *foldtogram (1152" x 50", August, iteration 3)* (p. 43)—comprised of an entire roll of RC glossy photo paper—in a plastic vat in their upstate New York studio.[14] As much performance as they are objects, Episalla's "foldtograms" are responses to substantial corporeal manipulation and heat, with expired chemicals applied in the "incorrect" order and light exposures happening at the "incorrect" times. A work's final thrust occurs with its installation, for which Episalla spends considerable time studying the architectural particularities of the space. Often beginning on the wall, the *foldtogram* eventually comes into contact with the floor, a surface that photographs do not commonly activate or encounter. This aliveness, further emboldened by its sheer mass, ensures the work's constant regeneration from space to space.

FORM

Parallel to discussions on scale, the concept of form has developed significantly since the medium's earliest years. In this section, form speaks to both the photograph's physical construction, as well as the conceptual devices that address form within the image. Whereas Iranian artist Gohar Dashti collects and disassembles botanical specimens for her large format prints, German artist Stefanie Seufert assembles physical structures using folded color photograms.

Although Dashti is best known for her documentary and large-scale, mise-en-scène format photographs, she paired the language of abstraction with cameraless processes to explore a distinct sense of place in her 2017 series *Still Life* (p. 67). Dashti chose to create photograms, as well as cyanotypes, which produce a punchy blue background resulting from the particular chemistry used in its processing. Dashti's personal history, especially her childhood in Iran, is the foundation of her nuanced practice. Born in Ahvaz—a historically contested city that sits on the border between Iran and Iraq—Dashti recalls mass flight from the city during the bombings and daily conflict of the Iran-Iraq War (1980–88). Despite these recollections, the artist has trouble summoning any real memories of her home, a core subject in her work. Themes of disconnection and displacement from home and country are woven throughout Dashti's dreamlike images of abandoned buildings that seemingly propagate soft wheat stalks and verdant flora. *Still Life* builds on these ideas through tightly cropped impressions of found plant matter that Dashti manipulated, distorted, and scattered across the photographic field. The already abstracted specimen—exemplified in the glass-like organic shards of *Untitled #14* (fig. 8)—is further abstracted from its original form through the act of destruction and subsequent disintegration. Although Dashti believes in nature's sustained power and centrality in conceptions of place, she also demonstrates the fragility and ephemerality of its physical forms.

Seufert, on the other hand, erects chromatic architectural structures of variable sizes within the gallery space. Akin to stele, each *Tower* (pp. 74–75) draws attention to the particularities of its form—vertical, geometric, and rigid featuring multiple, jewel-like facets that shine across its surfaces. In fact, the towers possess a lustrous and nearly lifelike presence. Seufert works in the darkroom by exposing and folding the paper, then repeating the process until she is satisfied with the outcome. The transition from flat and folded to modeled and monumental happens after development and fixing. Once constructed, the works are solid, but also appear to shift and bend in space, aspects that are further emphasized by the gradated impressions of crossing diagonals and layered diamond shapes. Each tower is also a product of individual movement

Fig. 8. Gohar Dashti (Iranian, b. 1980). *Untitled #14* from the series *Still Life*, 2017. Inkjet print, 38 x 47 ¼ in. (97 x 120 cm). Edition of 10 + 2AP. Courtesy of the artist

and manipulation. The glossy surfaces show viewers their dimples and imperfections, referring back to the body and labor of Seufert. Similarly, Seufert's titles reflect the *Towers'* individuality as if alluding to an almost consumer-driven model à la Pantone colors or fabric swatches, which has been addressed in other bodies of Seufert's work that explore pringles and dog toys. "Dark Aubergine," "Just Yellow," and "Atlas Grey," work to differentiate one form from another, implying options, choices, and the tendency to choose favorites. Seufert's *Towers* represent the play of form and color, whilst vibrating between photography, sculpture, and architecture.

TEXTURE

Considerations of texture in photography are usually limited to its purely visual variations and patterns: brittle and flaking tree bark, wrinkled skin, or staccato gusts of wind dimpling seawater. Throughout the exhibition, a wide range of surface qualities and textures are demonstrated through analogue processing techniques; however, the textural beyond mere depiction or reference, artists like Hernease Davis and Dakota Mace confront the boundaries of the medium, as well as our in-person experience of it.

American artist Davis finds comfort in physical and tactile experimentation. Her multimedia work is motivated by empathy and improvisation, ultimately providing a way to process emotional traumas through artistic production. By incorporating crocheted yarn, textiles, and sound installations, Davis builds palpable textures into her practice. Her method is one of the most critical aspects: for her series *Bare With Me, Foundation* (p. 58) the artist punctures the surface of the photograph to thread yarn—some treated with cyanotype chemistry, others are copper or deep brown in tone—through the object. In complete darkness, she crochets as she hums, using the length of the song as a limit for each "foundation chain," the first series of stitches that mark the beginning of any crochet project. The fact that her stitching is both improvised and in the darkness further fulfills the artist's therapeutic goals, and becomes a meaningful source

Fig. 9. Hernease Davis (American, b. 1982). *A Womb of My Own (Mistakes Were Made in Development)* (installation view, Visual Studies Workshop, Rochester, New York, USA, 2018). Courtesy of the artist

for learning how to slow down and let go. Following the crocheting, Davis rests her body atop the paper and meditates for as long as her intuition allows. Visually, the yarn suggests a form of "safety net," gently embracing each print with its thoughtfully woven fibers. Some of Davis's installations mirror this idea, wherein she includes crocheted blankets suspended from the ceiling and encircling a sound piece (fig. 9). In order to listen, one must enter the womb-like space within the gallery. For Davis, crocheting is also an extension of family tradition that was shared with her by her aunt, and was also established by a significant blanket given to Davis at age eighteen. Integrated into the artist's practice, this multisensory, textural experience acts as a method of self-soothing for Davis and viewers alike.

Diné (Navajo) artist Mace similarly embeds unexpected materials into her photographic objects. For her series *Náhookǫs Bikǫ'í* (pp. 60–61), Mace first creates a chemigram by splashing and splattering photographic developer or fixer onto a piece of light-sensitive paper in the incorrect order and method. Mace then punctures the photograph with a needle and hand sews a series of tiny glass beads and abalone shells through the surface of the print. Her chemigrams often feature Diné motifs, which the artist integrates as an examination of Navajo culture, heritage, and trade. Mace's previous work has addressed the cultural appropriation of designs and symbols of native cultures, specifically Navajo textile designs. She believes this type of appropriation contributes to the creation of a "hyperreality," or "a world of self-referential signs . . . which are infinitely reproducible and said to substitute for a 'real' or 'original' that does not now exist and perhaps never existed."[15] Simulating Navajo weaving techniques, Mace's intricate beadwork often reinterprets four symbols connected to the Diné creation story and deities. The addition of glass beads also addresses the European colonial introduction of glass to native cultures. Mace describes this as a kind of reclamation of cultural appropriation from white, Western culture. The tactile beads and shells provide texture, but also a method through which to complicate ideas surrounding cultural exchange, adoption, and appropriation.

VALUE

As an artistic element, value defines the lightness or darkness of a color based on a scale of white to black. However, for this exhibition, value embodies an adjacent spectrum: transparency to opacity, in both visual and conceptual readings. Indian-American artist Priya Suresh Kambli uses strategies of concealment and erasure—rendered as translucent and opaque abstract patterns—as a gesture of protection for worship objects. Employing an almost opposite strategy, South African artist Brent Meistre examines the liminal space of the window—illustrated as simultaneously transparent and opaque—as it relates to state-sanctioned violence, the surveyor, and the surveyed.

Kambli's ongoing series *Devhara* (p. 82), features installations of intricately patterned cyanotypes of fluctuating value across entire walls (fig. 10). A Marathi word, "Devhara" loosely translates to a kind of frame or enclosed case meant for an idol or shrine. When Kambli immigrated from India to the United States at the age of eighteen, she brought only as many personal items as she could fit into a suitcase; some of these included her father's family photographs and her mother's devotional objects. Similarly, after each visit to India since then, Kambli returns with a figure of a god that she then adds to her late mother's altar. Although the objects are personal to Kambli, they are also mass-produced, leading the artist to question how the meaning of objects shift when they are divorced from their origins. Considering their cultural and religious significance, Kambli determined it was crucial to find an alternative strategy to representation, as a protective measure from possible exoticization and fetishization. Thus, the cyanotype technique renders her mother's idols in negative format and abstracts them into circles, moons, stars, and ovals that harmonize together in large-scale patterns. Some materialize as brightly lit oculi, others as shaded floral arrangements. The broad range of translucent and opaque forms is achieved through meticulous layering under the natural sunlight that grazes her

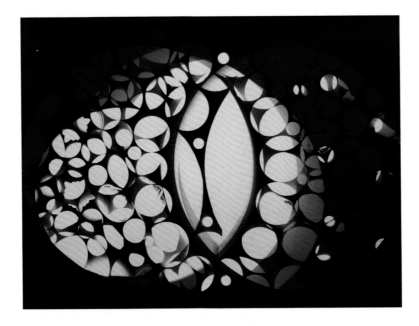

Fig. 10. Priya Suresh Kambli (Indian-American, b. 1975). *Devhara*, 2021. Cyanotype, 18 x 24 in. (45.7 x 61 cm). Courtesy of the artist

Midwestern backyard. Kambli arranges and rearranges each print several times, and dodges and burns using her own body. Depending upon the strength of the sun and the complexity of the pattern, each print requires anywhere from forty-five minutes to six hours to produce. Differing values are at the center of *Devhara*, through which Kambli intentionally erases and negates the objects not as a disparaging act, but rather as a preservational one.

Rather than obscuring cultural meaning, Meistre seeks to reveal its failures. Presented as a diptych, *Casspir Window* (p. 84) is a set of photograms that addresses the cultural memory of the South African Apartheid era (1948–94). The Casspir is a landmine-resistant armored military vehicle developed in the late 1970s for the protected transport of South African police troops. For many, its hulking eleven-ton, skillfully engineered body epitomizes the repressive racial segregation policies and resulting militant violence that defined the Apartheid era. Meistre selected the vehicle's deliberately small windows—which were used to survey and even open fire on crowds—to be the focal point of the work. In a sense, Meistre considers the Casspir a stand-in for the camera apparatus: military and police personnel peering through its small apertures to instill fear in and inflict violence upon their fellow people. Fractured, fissured, and bullet-ridden, Meistre's photogrammed window fragments depend upon subtle visual deviations in value. Sharply outlined with an opaque, jagged edge, each shattered section suggests transparency, but instead contrasts with descending shadows that act as a vignette around the object. In fact, the transparency that is ordinarily intrinsic to a window is actually negated by the black field resting beneath it. Meistre's *Casspir Window* is commentary on the state's dependence upon institutionalized vision as measures of intimidation, control, and obfuscation.

Through the work of forty-two global artists, *Direct Contact* demonstrates a wide stratum of engagement with photography's origins and selfhood. It is a stunning, contemporary capture of the sheer possibility that endures within this medium and beyond, further emphasizing that our questions about photography continue to be relevant, expand to new depths, and provoke innovative responses.

End

In 2017, the Olive Cotton Award—a biennial $20,000 award for Australian artistic excellence in photographic portraiture—was awarded to Justine Varga for her cameraless photograph *Maternal Line* (fig. 11). The decision erupted in a frenzy of controversy that extended internationally. The large-format print features a series of marks and doodles made on negative film with pen and saliva by Varga's Hungarian grandmother. *Maternal Line* could be perceived as unconventional on a few levels: it is a non-representational photograph, it is cameraless, and it "misuses" conventional materials, but also features surprising ones. It is also colossal; however, it is not meant to deceive or disorient. Varga offers clues regarding its physicality and enlargement by presenting the entire, spliced negative with visible sprockets along its top and bottom edges. None of these aspects, however, should be controversial.

Although conceptual at its foundation, Varga's photography depends heavily on grasping how materiality and process inform our experience of photography. Like other artists included in *Direct Contact*, she pokes and prods her film, accepting that she is abandoning the feeling of comprehensive control in her practice. Given Varga's embrace of materials like saliva and tears—or techniques like scratching, scribbling, and massaging—it is unsurprising that her work has received some criticism in light of photography's historical associations with precision and tradition. In many ways, a sense of preciousness still looms over photography, an unproductive and confounding position given the medium's omnipresence, myriad applications, and the history

Fig. 11. Justine Varga (Australian, b. 1984). *Maternal Line*, 2017. From the series *Photogenic Drawing*. Edition of 5. Chromogenic photograph, 61 ¹³⁄₁₆ x 48 in. (157 x 122 cm). Courtesy of the artist, Hugo Michell Gallery, Adelaide, and Tolarno Galleries, Melbourne

of art, writ large. However, it is exactly the unconventional and unrestricted nature of cameraless photographs that encourages viewers to both step into an unfamiliar realm and linger there. Without a dependence on representation, viewers are met with images that appear relatively unmediated. These objects demand more of our time and often ask more of our encounters with them, both precious commodities in today's world. Though we understand that no images, of any kind, can exist free of mediation, cameraless photographs plant some seeds of doubt. Yet, with increased exposure to those experiences that push us comes increased reflection, familiarity, and knowledge. The global artists featured in *Direct Contact* address all of these issues explicitly through material and process-oriented examinations of the photographic medium. With a heightened proximity to the physical world—touch, contact, and impression—perhaps cameraless photography brings viewers closer to "an art of the real."[16]

NOTES

1   Hagi Kenaan, *Photography and Its Shadow* (Stanford, CA: Stanford University Press, 2020), 12. Kenaan argues that in the present, human beings are "reluctant . . . to experience what is not intrinsically photographic." Considering the sheer ubiquity of photographic images, I employ "unphotographic" to differentiate cameraless from camera photographs.

2   Ariella Azoulay, "Photography—The Ontological Question," *Mafte/akh* 2e (2011): 65–80. Azoulay argues that the photograph is merely one outcome of the "event of photography," which she describes as a unique form of temporality first set in motion by the camera. The event is an infinite series of encounters that can happen between the camera, photographer, subject, and spectator, whether or not there is an awareness or physical presence of any such participant. The event of photography can never be terminated, given the endless potential for participation across space and time.

3   Latin for "dark chamber," camera obscura describes a dark room through which light enters a single, small hole. The camera obscura's earliest version dates back to antiquity, later becoming the predecessor of the photographic camera.

4   Jessica S. McDonald, "Introducing 'The Niépce Heliograph,'" *Harry Ransom Center Magazine*, University of Texas, Austin, last modified August 20, 2019, https://sites.utexas.edu/ransomcentermagazine/2019/08/20/introducing-the-niepce-heliograph/. Niépce's object is part of the Gernsheim Collection at the Harry Ransom Center at the University of Texas, Austin. Jessica S. McDonald, Nancy Inman and Marlene Nathan Meyerson Curator of Photography, posits that British collectors and historians Helmut and Alison Gernsheim were responsible for coining "The World's First Photograph," after they rediscovered the object in 1952, fifty years after its last public exhibition. Helmut Gernsheim, a respected photo historian, believed that "factual, realistic presentation" defined successful photographs. Thus, it is unsurprising that he was a major proponent of Niépce's photograph and serves as an important example of how hierarchical structures impact the writing and canonization of history.

5   Poet and founder of the Dada movement Tristan Tzara (Romanian, 1896–1963) first referred to Schad's photograms as "schadographs," in the March 1920 issue of *Dadaphone*. Man Ray would mimic this years later, referring to his own such works as "rayographs."

6   Christian Schad, quoted in Jill Lloyd and Michael Peppiatt, *Christian Schad and the Neue Sachlichkeit* (New York: Neue Galerie New York, 2003), 19.

7   Howard Bossen, *Henry Holmes Smith: Man of Light*, Studies in Photography, 1st edition (Ann Arbor, MI: UMI Research Press, 1983), 161n49. Even Hare could not recall why he brought Karo© corn syrup into the classroom; however, he acknowledged Smith's pivotal role in building the photography program at IU.

8   Wash-Off Relief Imbibition printing, with slight variations, became the dye transfer process after the Second World War. Often used in commercial printing and famously by Technicolor for color motion pictures, the process required at least three distinctive dye transfers; however, by the late 1930s Smith was already executing six to ten transfers. Dye transfer is largely unknown to today's viewers because Eastman Kodak discontinued production of the specialized materials and chemicals in 1994.

9   Betty Hahn, "Henry Holmes Smith: Speaking with a Genuine Voice," *Image* 16, no. 4 (December 1973): 3.

10 Olivier Lugon, "Photography and Scale: Projection, Exhibition, Collection," *Art History* (April 2015): 386–403.

11 See Michael Fried, *Why Photography Matters As Art As Never Before* (New Haven, CT: Yale University Press, 2008).

12 Huarcaya's projects have been in collaboration with and commissioned by the Wildlife Conservation Society and Rainforest Expeditions.

13 Joy Episalla, personal communication with the author, December 3, 2021.

14 RC, or resin-coated, glossy photo papers differ from other papers because the base is sealed between two polyethylene layers. This coating gives prints a lustrous, glossy finish.

15 Maureen Trudelle Schwarz, *Fighting Colonialism with Hegemonic Culture: Native American Appropriation of Indian Stereotypes* (Albany, NY: SUNY Press, 2013), 1. Hyperreality was initially conceptualized in the mid-1990s by Jean Baudrillard to explain the human inability to differentiate reality from a simulation of reality. See also Jean Baudrillard, *Simulacra and Simulation* (Ann Arbor: The University of Michigan Press, 1994).

16 Geoffrey Batchen, *Emanations: The Art of the Cameraless Photograph* (New York: Prestel, 2016), 5.

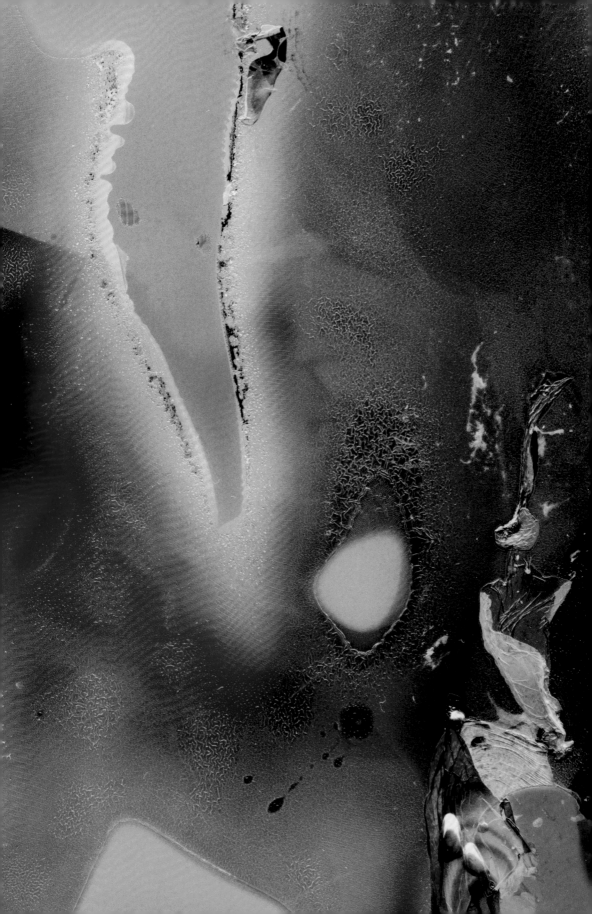

CATALOGUE

AGE

Addressing notions of age, decay, and expiration, these objects confront the role that time plays in the photographic event. Artists in this section work with unfixed, expired, or ephemeral photographic materials; found historic relics; confront timely notions of environmental decline; or aging and decay through explorations of disease and death.

Chris Duncan
American, b. 1974

Orange Skylight (6 Month Exposure), 2016
Acrylic paint and direct sunlight on fabric, 84 x 54 in. (213.4 x 137.2 cm)
Courtesy of the artist and Halsey McKay Gallery, East Hampton

For *Orange Skylight (6 Month Exposure)* Duncan merged architectural space, direct-sun exposure, manufactured fabric, and acrylic paint to investigate our perceptions of light and experience of time's physical and psychological effects. His employment of extremely long exposure times (six months to a year), sunlight, and natural elements—without any other chemical accelerant or emulsion—complicates any clear delineations between photography and painting.

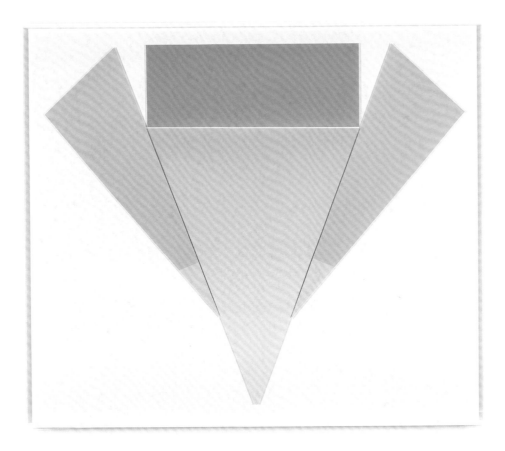

Amanda Marchand
Canadian, b. 1968

Pitcher's Thistle (Evolved), 2020
Edition 1/3, from the series *The World is Astonishing with You in It: A 21st Century Field Guide to the Birds, Ferns and Wildflowers*
Inkjet print collage, 4 panels, 44 x 52 x 2 ½ in. (111.8 x 132 x 6.4 cm)
Courtesy of the artist and Traywick Contemporary, Berkeley

Assembled as a collage, *Pitcher's Thistle (Evolved)* joins together four softly hued lumen prints made from black-and-white photographic paper in a hard-lined geometric form. Native to the sandy shorelines of the Great Lakes, pitcher's thistle was federally classified as a threatened species in 1996 due to increased disturbance of its habitat. Part of Marchand's larger series, *The World is Astonishing with You in It: A 21st Century Field Guide to the Birds, Ferns and Wildflowers*, *Pitcher's Thistle* reflects upon time and the human relationship to our planet and landscape.

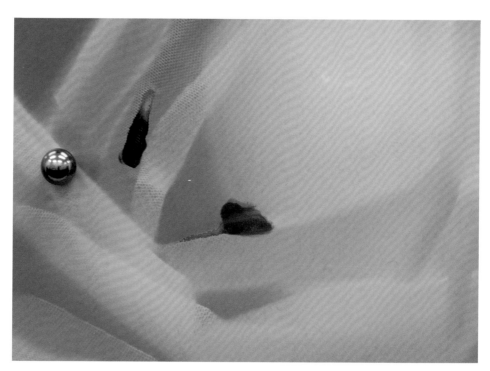

Laurie Kang
Korean-Canadian, b. 1985

Guts, 2019–21
Photograms, magnets, and silicone, 120 x 120 in. (304.8 x 304.8 cm)
Courtesy of the artist and Franz Kaka, Toronto

In *Guts*, Kang examined the "parasitic nature" of unfixed—or, continually developing—photographic objects and their broader relationship to a functioning body: photographic paper as flesh like, silicone as intestinal, and slow image development as a kind of digestive or metabolic process. A combination of scraps from sculptural casts and garbage that produces new objects, each component is the result of material cannibalism and regurgitation. Analogous to microscopic specimens, Kang's cloudy, pallid photograms seem to squirm across the silicone carrier.

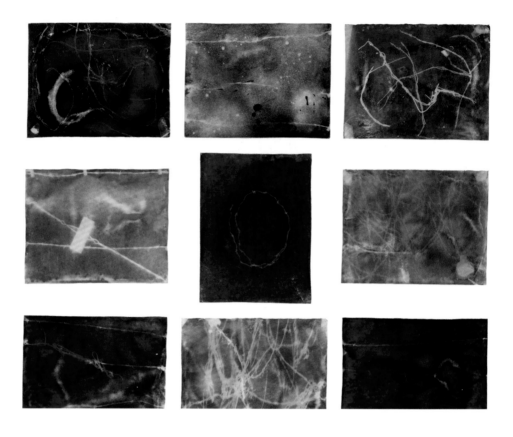

Osamu James Nakagawa
Japanese-American, b. 1962

9066 • Trace, 2022
Nine cyanotypes, 19 x 25 in. each; 61 x 79 in. overall (48.3 x 63.5 cm each, 154.9 x 200.7 cm overall)
Courtesy of the artist

For Nakagawa's most recent series, *9066 • Trace*, the artist visited the sites of former Japanese internment camps across the American West. He collected remnants from what remains of the camps—barbed wire, tin cans, and broken window glass—and coupled them with the cyanotype technique to examine this neglected period in American history that is an enduring, painful cultural memory. The number 9066 refers to U.S. President Franklin Roosevelt's 1942 executive order authorizing the forced evacuation and relocation of any persons based on the West Coast found to be a threat to national security. Though the language was intentionally vague, the order purposely targeted people of Japanese descent, resulting in the mass incarceration and loss of personal liberties, properties, and businesses of 122,000 Japanese-Americans, 70,000 of whom were U.S. citizens.

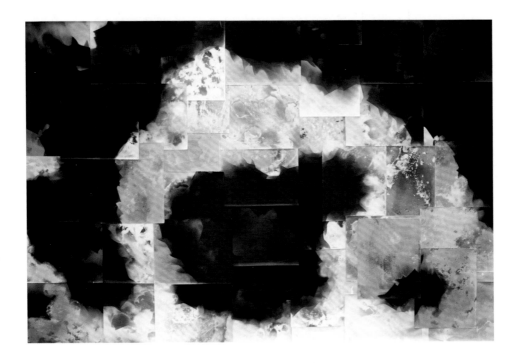

David Ondrik
American, b. 1976

Thrust, 2022
From the series *Inheritance*
Unique gelatin silver prints, 40 x 60 x 2 in. (101.6 x 152.4 x 5.1 cm)
Courtesy of the artist

Through the language of abstraction, Ondrik examines the emotional and physical magnitudes of terminal illness, and individual and communal loss. *Thrust*'s layers of unique, gelatin silver prints are chemically processed to intentionally activate soft, but muddied, ochres and lavenders from the otherwise black-and-white paper. After its assembly, *Thrust* mutates into a kind of noxious haze: Ondrik's metaphor for the all-consuming grief that follows witnessing a loved one's bodily decline.

Mariah Robertson
American, b. 1975

150 151, 2020
Unique chromogenic print, 50 x 66 in. (127 x 167.6 cm)
Courtesy of the artist and M+B, Los Angeles

150 151 displays a hypnotic array of irregularly shaped, brightly colored prints in a single blue frame. Contingent upon ideas of progression and repetition, Robertson worked across several intervals to create each hybrid work in this series. She used hand-cut dodging masks, controlled exposure times, and color filters to coax out the rich tonal ranges, then cut and re-integrated the prints together. Robertson's method collapses the idea of a photographic "instant" and explores these composites as both representation and object.

Anna Katharina Scheidegger
Swiss, b. 1976

Untitled, 2022
From the series *Melting Diamonds*
Chromogenic print on lightbox, 20 ½ x 26 ¾ x 32 in. (52 x 68 x 81.3 cm)
Courtesy of the artist

Scheidegger's ongoing series *Melting Diamonds* is a vibrant, mesmerizing record of coarse ice crystals across a flat plane. Each summer, Scheidegger travels to glaciers around the world to gather ice samples and create photograms in situ. Massive frozen landforms, glaciers symbolize a time before our own. Through the ice's ephemerality of the ice—which is further emphasized in their spectral formal qualities—Scheidegger challenges viewers to view *Melting Diamonds* as synecdoche of heightening climate change.

Assaf Shaham
Israeli, b. 1983

FR (300 DPI), 2012
From the series *Full Reflection*
Inkjet print, 42 ½ x 30 ¹¹⁄₁₆ in. (108 x 78 cm)
Courtesy of the artist and Braverman Gallery, Tel Aviv

To create *FR (300 DPI)*, Shaham positioned two flatbed scanners toward one another, simultaneously pressed "scan," and allowed their lights to reflect and refract off of the others' glass beds. Calling to mind De Stijl visual language, Shaham's "scanograms" are also an exercise in formal reduction. *FR (300 DPI)* is self-reflective, leading to questions about the conditions necessary to make photographs and exactly whom—or what—can record time.

Daisuke Yokota
Japanese, b. 1983

Untitled, 2015
Edition 2/6, from the series *Color Photographs*
Inkjet print, 14 ¼ x 17 ¾ in. (36.2 x 45.1 cm)
Museum purchase with funds from the Martha and David Moore Endowment for Prints,
Drawings and Photographs, Eskenazi Museum of Art, Indiana University, 2021.186

For Yokota's series *Color Photographs*, the physical aspects and material reactions of film are critical. Yokota stacked several strata of unused large-format color film, doused them with boiling water and other unorthodox development methods, and later scanned the results. *Untitled* is contradictory: at once melted and solid, transparent and opaque, and productive and deteriorating. Yokota describes his approach as a means for showing the impossible—"the accumulation of time" in a single photograph.

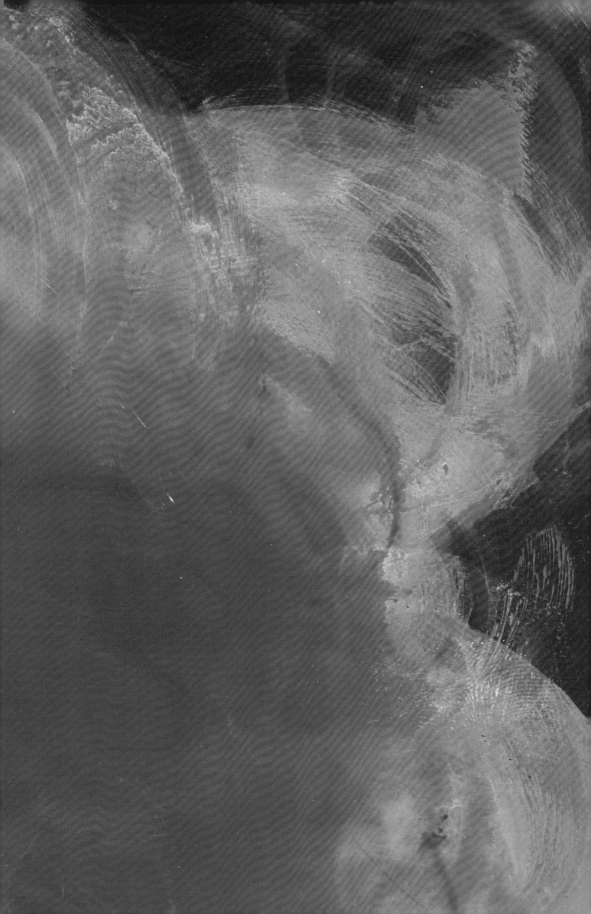

SCALE

Scale considers photography's multifaceted relationship with size, both in terms of display and representation. Objects in this section address scale as it applies to sculptural objects, the built and natural environments, and compositional devices used to encourage new ways for viewers to encounter and experience a photograph's physical dimensions.

Anthea Behm
Australian, b. 1977

Showing the Hand, 2016
Black-and-white silver gelatin photogram, 47 x 42 in. (119.4 x 106.7 cm)
Courtesy of the artist

Behm's work complicates notions of artistic, social, and institutional authenticity using the idea of "the artist's hand" as a point of departure. *Showing the Hand* presents an exaggerated, partial depiction of a hand, as it hovers both in and out of a pocket. Combining drawing and internet-sourced images with a highly controlled photogram process using black-and-white silver gelatin paper, Behm probed how pictorial signs garner meaning.

Joy Episalla
American, b. 1960

foldtogram (1152 " x 50", August, iteration 3), 2019/2021/2023
Silver gelatin object/photogram on Ilford Glossy RC, 1,152 x 50 in. (2,926.1 x 127 cm)
Courtesy of the artist

foldtogram—a hybrid of "folded" and "photogram"—underscores Episalla's impressive physical manipulations of sculptural objects in direct relationship to their architectural surroundings. This largescale photo-object defies many of the medium's typical analogue parameters: it is not reproducible; its emulsion layer is cracked, folded, burned, and utterly compromised; it favors the unfussy application of developer, stop bath, and fixer in no single order; and it is (mostly) emancipated from the wall. With each installation of foldtogram (1152" x 50", August), Episalla generates a new and distinctive iteration of the work.

This image shows the work as it was installed at ICA Philadelphia in 2019. The installation at the Eskenazi Museum of Art could not be photographed before the time of this publication.

Nikolai Ishchuk
British-Russian, b. 1982

Arcadia (3), 2018
Silver gelatin prints, cyanotype, oil stick, and mixed media, 40 ⅛ x 68 ½ x ¾ in. (101.9 x 174 x 2 cm)
Courtesy of the artist and Marshall Gallery, Santa Monica

In Ishchuk's ongoing series *Arcadia* he blends photography, drawing, painting, and other mixed media as a means of reimagining mountain vistas as geometric compositions. Drawing a visual connection to modernist architecture, Ishchuk's objects speak to how styles like Brutalism (steel frames, cantilevered designs, and colossal presence) dominate the natural landscape and embody a new iteration of the sublime.

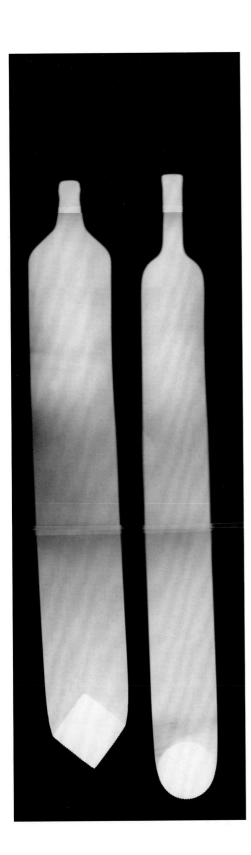

Julio Grinblatt
Argentinian, b. 1960

Photogram #015, 2015
From the series *Mirando Morandi*
Unique selenium-toned print,
34 x 10 ½ in. (86.4 x 26.7 cm)
Courtesy of the artist and
MINUS SPACE, Brooklyn

A reference to the prolific still life paintings
of Giorgio Morandi (Italian, 1890–1964),
Photogram #015 examines the relationship
between painting, photography, and
representation. By moving bottles across a
light-sensitive surface, Grinblatt performed
an indexical and performative "painting"
with objects and light. In doing so, he
connected Morandi's transformation of
mundane objects with the photogram's
similarly unforeseen evolution.

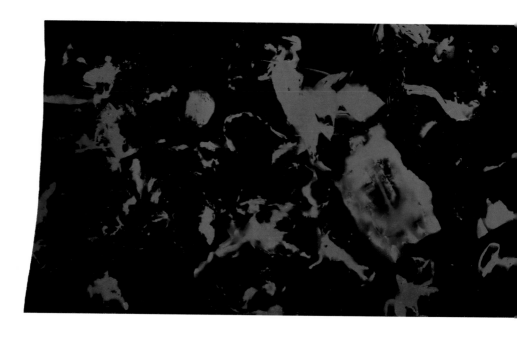

Roberto Huarcaya
Peruvian, b. 1959

Sea and Garbage (Mar y Basura I), 2018
From the series *Océanos*
Color photogram, 157 ½ x 42 ½ in. (400.1 x 108 cm)
Courtesy of the artist and ROLF Art, Buenos Aires

Working with chromogenic paper, seawater, and beach garbage collected by the artist and his family, Huarcaya generated an immersive, but unpredictable image of the landscape. Conjuring the irreversible damage caused by colorful plastics on the marine ecosystem, *Sea and Garbage (Mar y Basura I)* reflects on oceanic contamination, environmental destruction, and the part we all actively play in our earth's decline.

Fabiola Menchelli
Mexican, b. 1983

Horizon II, 2019
Edition 1/4
Inkjet print, 20 x 30 in. (51 x 76 cm)
Museum purchase with funds from the Jane Fortune Fund for Virtual Advancement
of Women Artists, Eskenazi Museum of Art, Indiana University, 2021.199

In her series *Horizons*, Menchelli explores what she calls, "the poetics of the edge," by focusing on and
enlarging the velvet threshold found on 35mm film canisters. By examining the physicality of the film's
container, Menchelli introduced a conceptual metaphor: perhaps the photograph acts as the container in
which we can observe ourselves as part of the world.

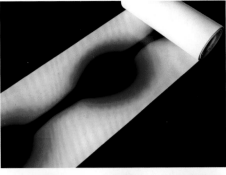

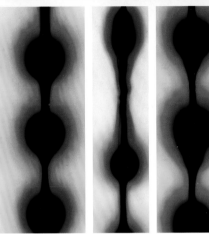

Kei Ito
Japanese, b. 1991

Sungazing Scroll, 2022
Chromogenic prints, wood, and metal
pipe, 12 x 2,160 in. (30.5 x 5,486.4 cm)
Museum purchase with funds from the Elisabeth P.
Myers Art Acquisition Endowment Fund, Eskenazi
Museum of Art, Indiana University, 2022.246

Sungazing Scroll is an ongoing series by Ito that
explores the historical memory of nuclear warfare
in Japan through his own generational trauma.
Using his grandfather's survival of the Hiroshima
atomic bomb attack as a point of departure,
Ito expels 108 breaths across a 200-foot-long
scroll of photographic paper in total darkness.
Simultaneously, he exposes the paper to sunlight
through a small aperture in the wall. Carrying ritual
significance in Japanese Buddhism, the number
108 is thought to deter evil and encourage healing.

*This image shows the work as it was installed at
another location. The installation at the Eskenazi
Museum of Art could not be photographed before
the time of this publication.*

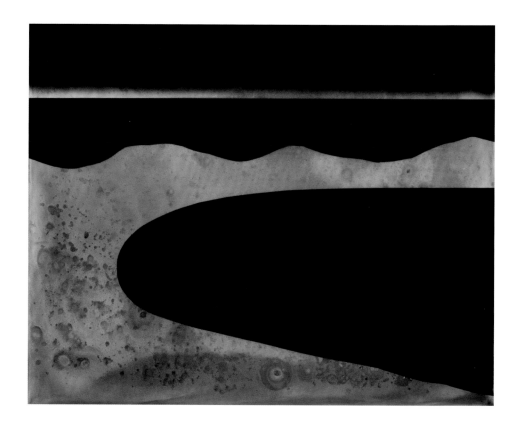

Nadezda Nikolova
Croatian-Bulgarian-American, b. 1978

Elemental Forms: Landscape no. 100, 2019
Unique wet plate collodion, 8 x 10 in. (20.3 x 25.4 cm)
Museum purchase with funds from the Martha and David Moore Endowment for Prints,
Drawings, and Photographs, Eskenazi Museum of Art, Indiana University, 2022.40

In *Elemental Forms, Landscape no. 100*, Nikolova considered how we experience, perceive, and impact the landscape around us. Using light, chemistry, cut paper, paint brushes, and cliché-verre, Nikolova distills her conception of a landscape into a unique cameraless composition on tin that gestures toward both abstraction and representation, and stillness and movement.

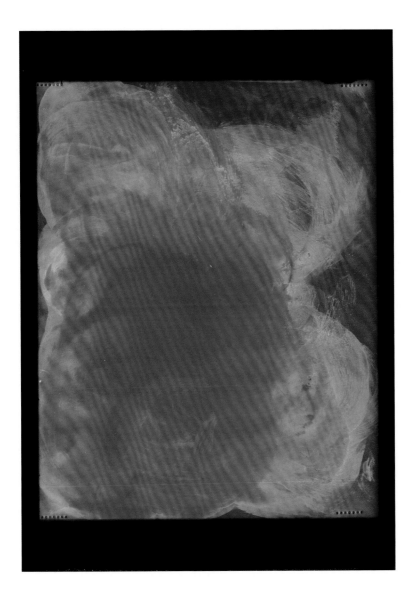

Justine Varga
Australian, b. 1984

Masseuse, 2017
Edition of 5 + 2AP, from the series *Photogenic Drawing*
Chromogenic photograph, 67 ¹⁵/₁₆ x 48 in. (172.5 x 122 cm)
Courtesy of the artist, Hugo Michell Gallery, Adelaide, and Tolarno Galleries, Melbourne

Autobiographical in nature, *Masseuse* is the haptic recording of Varga's paint-coated fingers massaging the emulsion of a negative in a reference to cliché verre. The larger series, *Photogenic Drawing*, is defined by Varga's intense physical labor, which involves spending hours in the darkroom and test printing on more than 750 feet of photographic paper. Commanded by an enormous and hypnotic fuchsia smear across the entire field, *Masseuse* examines photography's materiality and relationship to painting through the act of inscription.

TEXTURE

Topographical, woven, stitched, beaded, and coated, the objects in this section examine how texture informs the experience and interpretation of photographic objects. Texture is investigated beyond purely visual reference and instead focuses on the object's tactility and materiality, as well as conceptual structure and character.

1

Ellen Carey
American, b. 1952

1. **Dings & Shadows**, 2017
   Color photogram, 24 x 20 in. (61 x 50.8 cm)
   Museum purchase with funds from the
   Martha and David Moore Endowment for
   Prints, Drawings, and Photographs, Eskenazi
   Museum of Art, Indiana University, 2021.166

2. **Caesura**, 2016
   Color photogram, 24 x 20 in. (61 x 50.8 cm)
   Museum purchase with funds from the
   Martha and David Moore Endowment for
   Prints, Drawings, and Photographs, Eskenazi
   Museum of Art, Indiana University, 2021.167

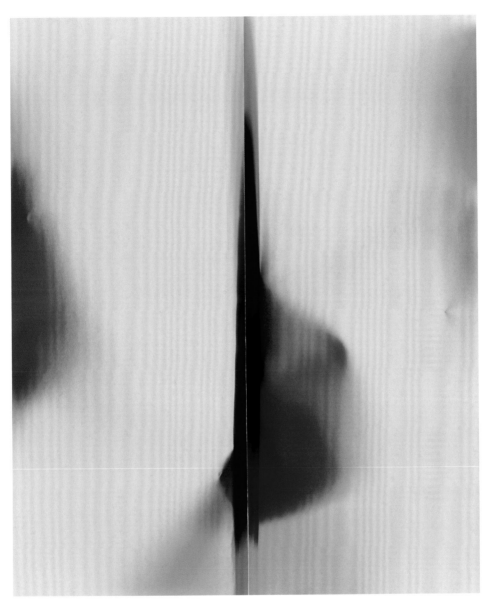

2

Reconsiderations of the traditional photogram, *Dings & Shadows* and *Caesura* are abstractions absent of any subject at all. Working in complete darkness, Carey first manipulated the light-sensitive paper and then introduced selective exposures by streaming light through various color filters. Cultivating both chance and intuition, Carey's photograms are topographical, prismatic displays of form, color, and volume, as well as a celebration of material. Carey often describes her conceptual practice as "photography degree zero" (a reference to Roland Barthes's *Writing Degree Zero*), or an ongoing effort to untether photography from its longstanding ties to representation.

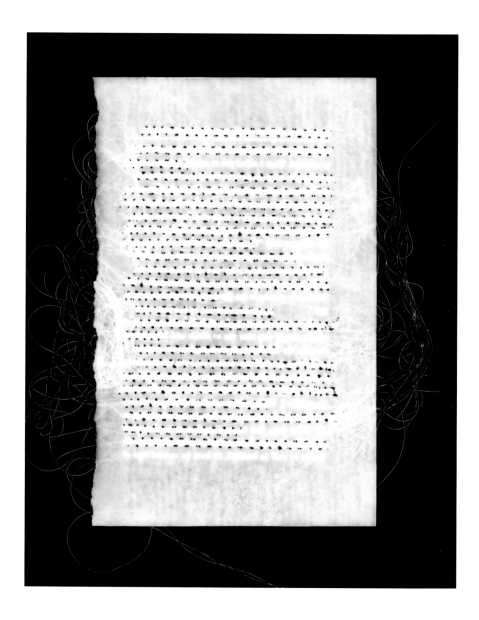

Elizabeth M. Claffey
American, b. 1980

Archived Attempts 1, 2022
Inkjet print, 43 x 53 in. (109.2 x 134.6 cm)
Courtesy of the artist

In *Archived Attempts 1*, Claffey scrutinized our contemporary relationship with canonical texts such as Ernest Hemingway's *The Old Man and the Sea* (1951). Through deliberate acts of redaction, the artist interrogated Hemingway's position of power and authorial appropriation of Cuban cultural perspectives and identities. Amidst Claffey's stitches, faint fragments of Hemingway's words appear across the page, reconstructed as a means of poetic action.

Judith Nangala Crispin
Australian–Bpangerang/Gunaikurnai, b. 1970

Melissa singing from inside the storm, over Brown Mountain, lulling white eucalypts to sleep, 2019
Lumachrome glass print, cliché verre, chemigram, roadkill Eastern Brown snake, sticks, dried leaves, shed python skin, and clay on fiber paper, exposed 32 hours in full summer light, 26 ³⁄₈ x 17 in. (67 x 43.2 cm)
Gift of the artist, 2022.247

Crispin works primarily with deceased animals as a means of reframing our human relationship to origin and death. For this work, she arranged an Eastern brown snake and other materials found in situ on top of light-sensitive paper, painted it with photochemistry, and exposed it to sunlight for thirty-two hours. She then overlaid a cliché-verre plate incised with drawn details to better visualize the animal's face. These "after life portraits" record light passing through the body of the animal to both honor spiritualism and country, as well as memorialize lives lost.

Hernease Davis
American, b. 1982

Bare with Me, Foundation, 17, 2021
From the series *A Womb of My Own (Mistakes Were Made in Development)*
Silver gelatin fiber photogram, crocheted yarn, cyanotype, 16 x 20 in. (40.6 x 50.8 cm)
Museum purchase with funds from the Jane Fortune Fund for Virtual Advancement
of Women Artists, Eskenazi Museum of Art, Indiana University, 2021.168

Davis's ongoing photogram series, *A Womb of My Own (Mistakes Were Made in Development)*, addresses both personal and familial trauma through empathic, process-oriented image-making. In darkness, she lays nude atop unexposed sheets of light-sensitive paper, embracing the unplanned and the improvised to create a long exposure as a method of healing. With the addition of crocheted yarn that has been treated with cyanotype chemicals, Davis creates a protective netting for each print that gestures toward ideas of care and preservation.

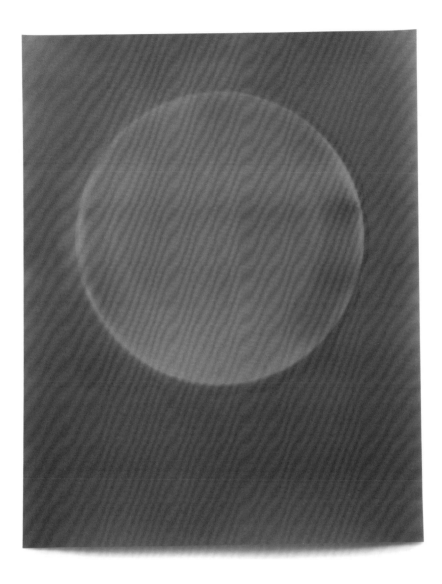

Galina Kurlat
Russian Jewish-American, b. 1981

September 18 (Used Bathwater), 2021
From the series *Charting the Hours*
Unique gelatin silver print, 16 x 20 in. (40.6 x 50.8 cm)
Courtesy of the artist

During the COVID-19 pandemic lockdown, Kurlat began *Charting the Hours*, a lumen print series born of the only materials available to her at the time: hair, saliva, blood, urine, and nail clippings. By integrating bodily matter and intentionally misusing the black-and-white paper through extended exposures and shifts in lighting, Kurlat accessed an array of muted nudes, iridescent mauves, and lipstick pinks. *September 18* features Kurlat and her partner's used bathwater as an index of their bodies, disruption of the photographic process, and subversion of the medium's representational impulse.

Dakota Mace
Diné, b. 1991

Náhookǫs Bikǫ' I, 2022
Chemigram, glass beads, and abalone shell
11 x 14 in. each, 20 ½ x 24 ¼ in. each (framed) (27.9 x 35.6 cm each; 52.1 x 61.6 cm framed)
Courtesy of the artist and Bruce Silverstein Gallery, New York

Drawing connections to her own Diné (Navajo) culture, memory, and landscape, in *Náhookǫs Bikǫ´ I* ("Polaris" in Navajo) Mace features intricate glass beadwork and abalone shell over motifs painted with photographic developer and fixer. Initially introduced to Native communities by European colonists, glass—specifically glass beads—became an integral material for trade. Mace's painstaking application of beads and shell references histories of labor and process-based artmaking.

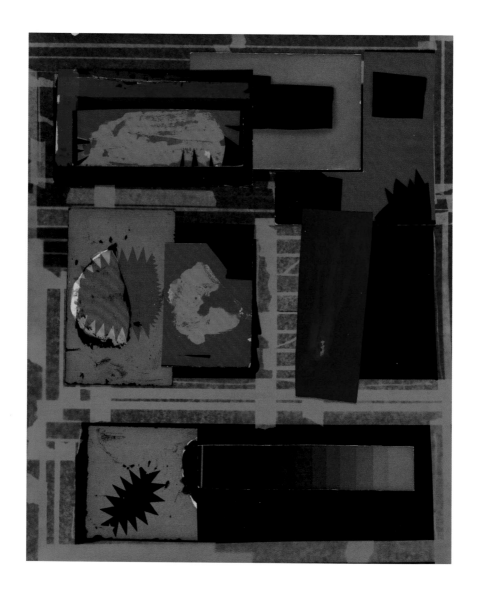

Aspen Mays
American, b. 1980

Hugo 21, 2019
Gelatin silver print, photogram, and green sintra, 26 x 22 in. (66 x 55.9 cm)
Museum purchase with funds from the Jane Fortune Fund for Virtual Advancement
of Women Artists, Eskenazi Museum of Art, Indiana University, 2021.165

In 1989, Hurricane Hugo devastated parts of Puerto Rico, the Caribbean islands St. Croix and Guadeloupe, and Charleston, South Carolina, Mays's hometown. In her series *Hugo*, Mays layered paper cutouts and created several exposures, referencing the vibrant, color-coded emergency maps and Doppler radar images so prevalent in the media. She also recreated one of her most distinct personal memories and one that dominated news coverage: the protective—but ultimately futile—ritual of taping windows before the storm's arrival. As such, Mays's photograms use the language of abstraction to investigate the human relationship with nature.

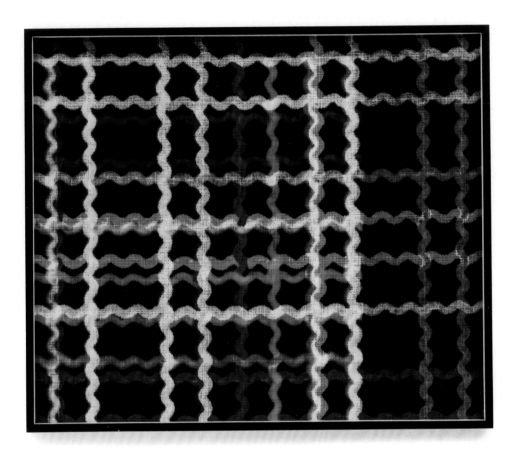

Lisa Oppenheim
American, b. 1975

Remnant (After Moholy), 2017
Edition of 1 + 1AP
Chromogenic print, 27 ⅞ x 33 ⅛ in. (70.8 x 84.1 cm)
Courtesy of the artist and Tanya Bonakdar Gallery, New York

Remnant (After Moholy) presents a black field vibrating with intersecting chromatic squiggles, almost
polyphonic in its appearance. By placing fabric directly onto a photographic enlarger, Oppenheim created a
hyper-enlarged, negative image that completely removed the textile's referent from the picture plane. Related
to a larger series on Lewis Hines's photographs of early twentieth-century child factory labor, Oppenheim
sourced vintage textiles from the same period to re-examine that history and its relevance to the present.

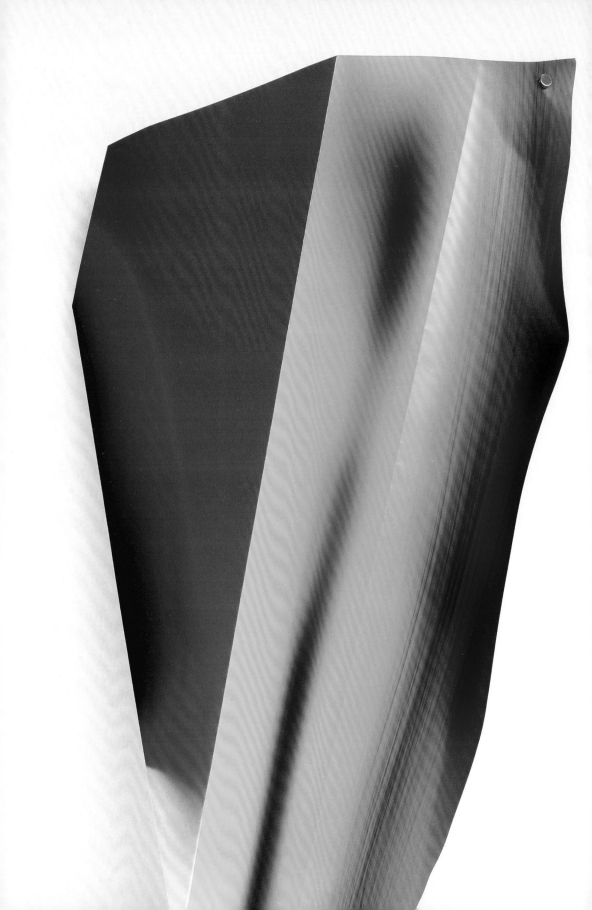

FORM

Form considers structures and bodies, both physical
and conceptual, as they relate to the photographic
medium. Objects featured in this section examine
physical construction and unconventional materials,
compositional devices related to form and formlessless,
and experimental formats of presentation and display.

Jillian Marie Browning
American, b. 1989

Matriarchal Line, 2018
30 cyanotypes on cotton fabric and wooden embroidery hoops, variable sizes
Courtesy of the artist

Referencing the studies of British botanist Anna Atkins, *Matriarchal Line* combines the cyanotype technique with the hair of the artist, their sisters, and their mother. With a likeness to DNA, each strand of hair—displayed in a gestural arrangement of round, wooden embroidery hoops—references a scientific specimen. Using their own family as proxy, Browning confronts the historical and scientific exploitation of Black women's bodies, as well as broader histories of domesticity and labor.

Gohar Dashti
Iranian, b. 1980

Untitled #3, 2017
Edition of 10 + 2AP, from the series *Still Life*
Inkjet print, 47 ⅕ x 47 ⅕ in. (120 x 120 cm)
Courtesy of the artist

In her series *Still Life* Dashti considered Iran's entanglement with histories of violence and war. Collecting organic materials from Tehran, Dashti manipulated and destroyed them to create cyanotypes of their shattered forms. A reference to early photographic taxonomies, Dashti's dynamic contact prints instead "suspend their subjects in a state of decay."

1

2

Marta Djourina
Bulgarian-German, b. 1991

1. **Untitled**, 2022
   From the series *Folds I*
   Direct exposure on folded,
   glossy analogue photo paper,
   22 ⁷/₁₆ x 27 ¹⁵/₁₆ x 7 ½ in.
   (57 x 71 x 19 cm)
   Courtesy of the artist

2. **Untitled**, 2020
   From the series *Folds I*
   Direct exposure on folded,
   glossy analogue photo paper,
   20 ¹/₁₆ x 29 ⅛ x 7 ½ in.
   (51 x 74 x 19 cm)
   Museum purchase with funds
   from the Martha and David
   Moore Endowment for Prints,
   Drawings, and Photographs,
   Eskenazi Museum of Art,
   Indiana University, 2021.187

3. **Untitled**, 2022
   From the series *Folds I*
   Direct exposure
   on folded, glossy
   analogue photo paper,
   48 ¹³/₁₆ x 14 ¹⁵/₁₆ x 7 ½ in.
   (124 x 38 x 19 cm)
   Courtesy of the artist

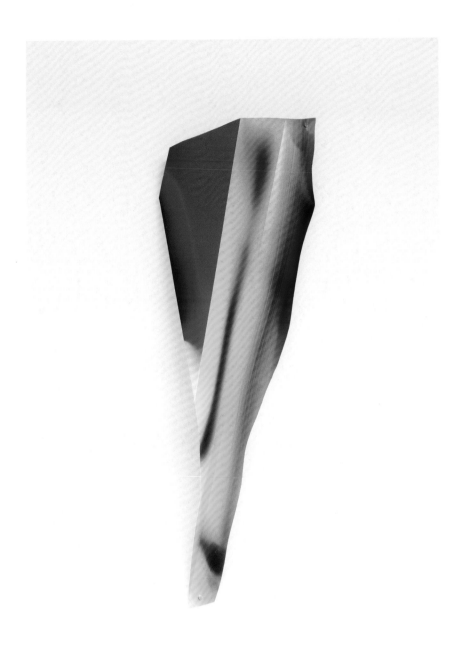

3

Djourina experiments with photographic abstraction through entirely bespoke means: "negatives" made only with her fingers, paint, and transparencies, and a homemade light-emitting diode connected to a battery pack around her waist. For these "blind-light paintings," Djourina worked in complete darkness. She first folded the light-sensitive paper and exposed it while moving around the LED device, essentially recording light's journey across the three-dimensional object.

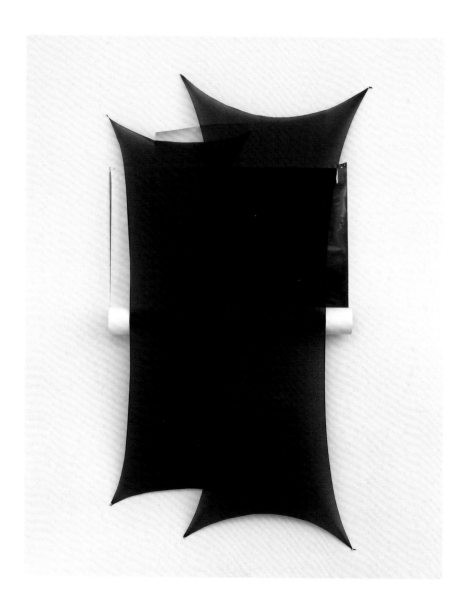

Sheree Hovsepian
Iranian-American, b. 1974

Material Gestures (A Meditation on Latency), 2016
Silver gelatin photogram, drawing paper, fabric, and pins, dimensions variable
Courtesy of the artist and Halsey McKay Gallery, East Hampton

As the title suggests, *Material Gestures (A Meditation on Latency)* examines the performative and bodily nature of darkroom work through a combination of drawing, photography, and sculptural assemblage. Hovsepian's use of stretched nylon references the artist's human scale and related choreography: the haptic concealment and exposure of light-sensitive paper using her body, opaque paper cutouts, and other handmade materials. Central to Hovsepian's work is the notion of play, a provocation of the precision and control historically associated with photography.

Tatiana Kronberg
American, b. Ukraine, 1979

Untitled, 2022
Chromogenic photogram, 30 x 52 in. (76.2 x 132.1 cm)
Courtesy of the artist

Nearly toppling outside of the confines of the frame, *Untitled* features a translucent, green body that is stiff, headless, and mannequin-like in appearance. Layered beneath is the less distinct yellow contour of a similar human-scale figure. Encased by floating silhouetted objects—a pair of scissors and enigmatic circular rings—Kronberg's disorienting photogram draws attention to the improvisational and active elements of image making.

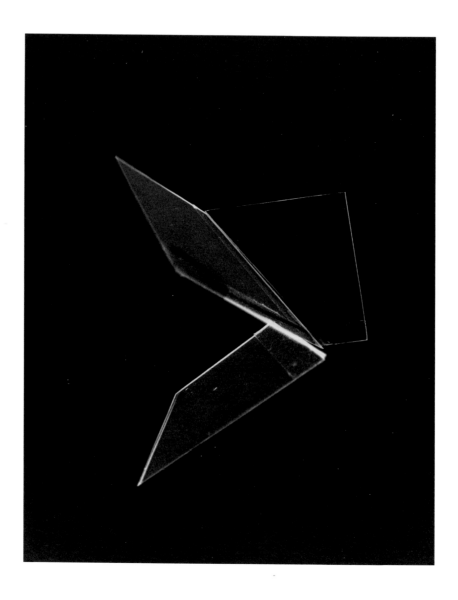

Letícia Ramos
Brazilian, b. 1976

Bichos Quadrados VI, 2019
Silver print photogram, 15 ¾ x 19 ¾ in. (40 x 50.2 cm)
Museum purchase with funds from the Jane Fortune Fund for Virtual Advancement
of Women Artists, Eskenazi Museum of Art, Indiana University, 2022.2

In *Bichos Quadrados VI*, Ramos examined spatial perception and the trajectory of light in photography. *Bicho*, Portuguese for "critter" or "creature," references the work of Neo-Concrete artist Lygia Clark (Brazilian, 1920–1988), whose 1960s hinged aluminum sculpture series by the same name encouraged viewer manipulation. Using transparent material, Ramos made her own versions of *Bichos*, in which she created an exposure on light-sensitive paper. Folding into and projecting outward from the photographic plane, Ramos considered light's role in manufacturing surface and volume.

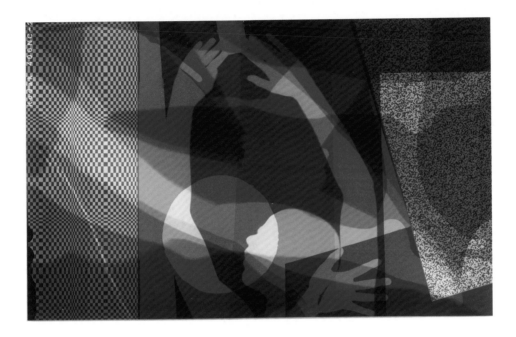

David Benjamin Sherry
American, b. 1981

Submission, OC100M160Y, 2017
From the series *Pink Genesis*
Color darkroom photogram, 29 ¾ x 47 ½ in. (75.6 x 120.7 cm)
Courtesy of the artist and Morán Morán Gallery, Los Angeles

Celebrating the darkroom as a transformative space, *Submission, OC100M160Y* is the result of a dynamic, unaccompanied performance in complete darkness. Depending upon years of learned technical choreography, Sherry alternated layering his own nude body with handmade stencils and props underneath a photographic enlarger. He intentionally merged the representational with the abstract as a queer strategy—a kind of genre code-switching—while also referencing a sense of eroticism grounded by touch.

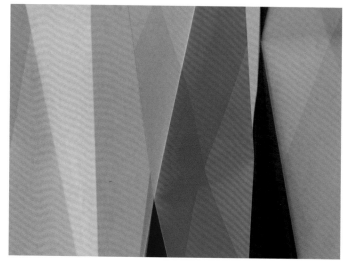

Stefanie Seufert
German, b. 1969

Towers (Dark Aubergine, Just Yellow, Atlas Grey), 2016/2021
Five photograms on Fuji color glossy paper, folded before
exposure, three: 71 x 14 x 14 in. each (180 x 35 x 35 cm each);
two: 52 x 10 x 10 in. each (130 x 25 x 25 cm each)
Courtesy of the artist and Laura Mars Gallery, Berlin

Hovering between "sculptural images and pictorial sculptures," the
works evoke a sense of authority more often afforded to architecture.
In the darkroom, Seufert first folded a sheet of light-sensitive paper,
then made an exposure, and repeated the process until she achieved
each delicate eggplant, yellow, and gray gradation.

*This image shows the work as it was installed at another location. The
installation at the Eskenazi Museum of Art could not be photographed
before the time of this publication.*

VALUE

Whereas "value" ordinarily defines the range from white
to black in art making, value as it applies to this exhibition
denotes a parallel range from transparent to opaque.
Artists employ these qualities to conceal, expose, and layer,
often generating conceptual links to historical legibility/
illegibility, institutional critique, and notions of visibility.

Yto Barrada
Moroccan-French, b. 1971

Bonbon 2, 2017
Photogram, 10 x 8 in. (25.4 x 20.3 cm)
Museum purchase with funds from the Jane Fortune Fund for Virtual Advancement
of Women Artists, Eskenazi Museum of Art, Indiana University, 2021.185

For her series *Bonbon*, Barrada selects pieces of wrapped candies native to her hometown of Tangier, Morocco,
and arranges them on light-sensitive paper. After exposure and development, the resulting abstract image
draws attention to themes of both absence and presence. Barrada has long expressed interest in how and by
whom history is written and how this relates to individual and familial experiences. Her work often focuses on
Morocco's colonial history, economics, and education through photography, film, sculpture, and installation.

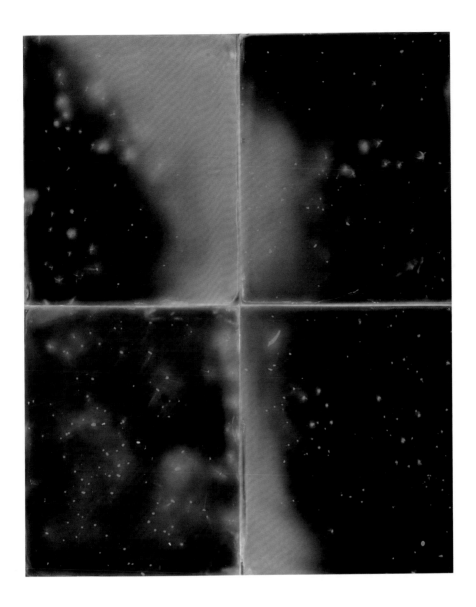

Granville Carroll
American, b. 1992

Untitled, 2020
From the series *Cosmotypes*
Inkjet print from collodion plate photogram, 16 x 20 in. (40.6 x 50.8 cm)
Courtesy of the artist

Carroll's series *Cosmotypes* is a poetic meditation on humanity's beginnings and the associated anxieties of existential unknowns. Using the wet collodion process, he coated aluminum, glass, and acrylic plates with collodion and streamed light through punctured foil sheets touching the otherwise darkened field. Informed by Afrofuturist thought, Carroll's work reclaims the universe's blackness—spatial, racial, spiritual, and temporal—as a strategy for generating new space, power, and futures from within the void.

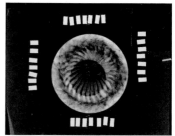

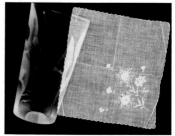

Iñaki Bonillas
Mexican, b. 1981

Secretos: rayografías, 2016
Five silver gelatin prints on fiber paper and walnut cabinet, 20 x 40 in. each (50.8 x 101.6 cm each)
Courtesy of the artist and gallery ProjecteSD, Barcelona

Secretos: rayografías is an examination of invisible and concealed spaces found in Casa Barragán, the spare Mexico City home designed and occupied by architect Luis Barragán. Compelled by the architect's intention to evoke harmony and balance, Bonillas revealed the parts of everyday life—its accumulations, junk, disorder, and even human emotions—that the architect sought to diminish from sight.

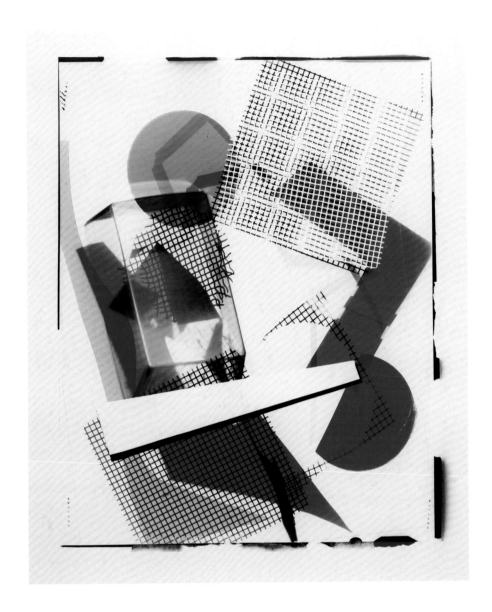

Danica Chappell
Australian, b. 1972

Moving Margin #2, 2020
Chromogenic photograph, 42 x 34 in. (106.7 x 86.4 cm)
Courtesy of the artist and Sous les Étoiles Gallery, New York

Combining experimental collage and non-representational imagery, *Moving Margins #2* plays with our senses of both proximity and distance. By employing tactile darkroom techniques like layering and collision, Chappell produced what she terms "spatial-temporal abstraction," a negotiation of movement, geometry, and play. With dynamic colors, forms, and textures, Chappell's work seeks to challenge preconceptions about photography's visual language.

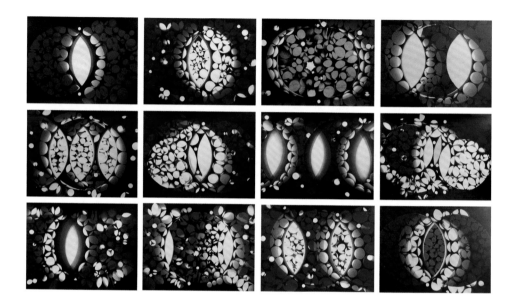

Priya Suresh Kambli
Indian-American, b. 1975

Devhara, 2020
Twelve cyanotypes, 18 x 24 in. each (45.7 x 61 cm each);
58 x 102 in. overall (147.3 x 259.1 cm overall)
Courtesy of the artist

Kambli's ongoing series *Devhara* ("house of idols" in Marathi) considers three generations of women (the artist, her mother, and her daughter) as they relate to migration, memory, and visual prayer. Kambli selects and places her mother's objects of worship atop cyanotype paper and exposes them to natural sunlight for several hours. Through the silhouettes made by this cameraless process, Kambli "re-appropriates abstraction from western modernism" to both obscure and protect her migrant identity and narrative.

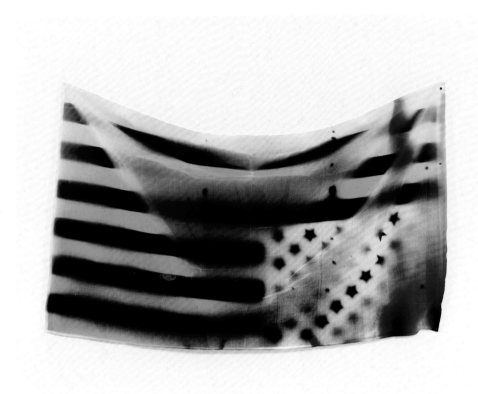

Farrah Karapetian
American, b. 1978

Distress Day 1, 2017
From the series *Flags & Teleprompters*
Chromogenic photogram, 39 x 55 in. (99.1 x 139.7 cm)
Courtesy of Nathan Laurell and Kristin McCoy

Following the 2016 election of Donald J. Trump to the office of U.S. president, Karapetian began probing symbols of American nationhood: the flag, the teleprompter, and the language of protest. *Distress Day 1* addresses the ongoing division and breakdown of civil discourse in the United States by inverting and making translucent the country's most recognizable symbol.

Brent Meistre
South African, b. 1975

Casspir Window, 2017
Two silver gelatin photograms, 20 x 24 in. each (50.8 x 61 cm each)
Courtesy of the artist

In *Casspir Window*, Meistre produced photograms of internal and external views from the bullet-ridden, shattered windows of a former South African mine-resistant ambush protected vehicle. Summoning a metaphor for the camera, the Apartheid-era vehicle's windows do not, in fact, reveal anything beyond them. In this way, Meistre posed questions about police violence, structures of power, and the memory of Apartheid in South Africa.

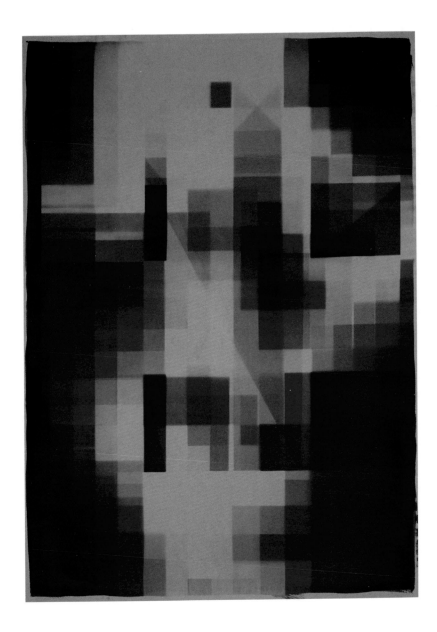

Iswanto Soerjanto
Indonesian, b. 1967

Kamadhatu, 2018
Cyanotype, 21 ¼ x 29 ½ in. (54 x 74.9 cm)
Courtesy of the artist and Gallery Lukisan, Bergen op Zoom, Netherlands

In *Kamadhatu* (Sanskrit for "sphere of desires"), Soerjanto combined abstraction and subtle gradations as a meditation on the origins, meaning, and potential binds of passion and desire. One of three realms in Buddhist spatial cosmology, *kamadhatu* is home to beings governed completely by sexual desire. Soerjanto based this work on the numerous relief panels depicting the realm of desire at the base of Java's Borobudur temples.

Glossary

Camera obscura

Latin for "dark chamber," **camera obscura** refers to a darkened room or box with a small hole or lens at one side, through which an image of the exterior scene is projected on the opposite interior wall of the device. Camera obscuras were used as scientific tools and drawing aids before the advent of photography; following the development of the photographic process in the early nineteenth century, the camera obscura formed the foundation of the modern camera.

Chemigram

A **chemigram** is an alternative photographic process in which photographic developer or fixer is applied to light-sensitive paper in full light. The resulting abstract compositions are comprised of black and white tones. Many artists apply other materials like wax, varnish, or nail polish prior to photographic chemistry to create organic patterns. Chemigrams are distinct from the related "chemogram," as the latter makes use of a traditionally exposed and enlarged photographic image as a base onto which chemicals are applied in the light.

Chromogenic print

A form of color photographic print, **chromogenic prints** use three layers of colored dye (cyan, magenta, and yellow) suspended in gelatin to produce a full-color image. Chromogenic prints, or c-type prints, were the major color print process of the twentieth century.

Cliché-verre

Invented in 1853 by Adalbert Cuvelier (French, 1812–1871) and Jean-Gabriel-Léandre Grandguillaume (French, 1807–1885), the **cliché-verre** was a short-lived artistic medium that combined existing printmaking techniques with the emerging photographic process. An artist makes a design on a glass plate, either by incising the design into an opaque layer or through the positive application of pigment to the plate. A print is made by placing the plate in contact with light-sensitive paper and exposing it to light. Multiple identical prints can be produced in this manner.

Collodion process (or wet-collodion process)

Invented in 1851 by Frederick Scott Archer (English, 1813–1857), the **collodion process** was an early innovation in photographic development. It would later form the basis for ambrotypes and tintypes, two popular forms of late-nineteenth-century plate photography. The process involves coating a glass plate in cellulose nitrate then immersing it in a solution of silver nitrate; the still-wet plate is then exposed in a camera. After exposure, the plate is developed using pyrogallic acid and fixed with a solution of sodium thiosulfate or potassium cyanide.

Contact print

A **contact print** is a photographic print made by placing a photographic negative in direct contact with light-sensitive paper and exposing it in that manner. This results in a printed image that is the same size as its corresponding negative. Photographers frequently make use of the contact print as an aid in the printing process to test exposure and development times before producing a full-size print.

Cyanotype

Invented by Sir John Herschel (English, 1792–1871) in 1842 and made popular by Anna Atkins shortly thereafter, a **cyanotype** is one of the earliest examples of a contact print. A sheet of paper is coated in light-sensitive iron salts and left to dry in the dark. An object (for example, a plant specimen) is then placed on top of the paper and left in direct sunlight for around fifteen to twenty minutes. Once the object is removed, its white silhouette is visible against a vibrant blue background and once washed with water, will remain fixed. The characteristic cyan blue hue is the result of ferric ammonium citrate and potassium ferricyanide.

"Dodging and burning"

"Dodging and burning" refers to two related interventions in the darkroom photographic printing process. Dodging concerns decreasing the exposure of a specific portion of the image to make it lighter, whereas burning refers to increasing the exposure of a specific portion to make it darker.

Dye transfer print

In use from the early to mid-twentieth century, the **dye transfer process** was a full-color photographic printing method in which three layers of colored dye (cyan, magenta, and yellow) were applied to a single emulsion using three separate color film matrices. The process was praised for its stability, saturation, and high color fidelity, but it was difficult to execute. The materials required to make a dye transfer print were discontinued by the Eastman Kodak Company in 1994.

Gelatin silver print

Gelatin silver is the most common chemical process used in modern black-and-white photographic printing. It relies on the suspension of light-sensitive silver halide crystals in a gelatin emulsion coated on paper.

Heliograph

Invented by Joseph Nicéphore Niépce (French, 1765–1833) in 1822, a **heliograph** is one of the earliest known photographic processes. It inspired the development of the daguerreotype and involves the exposure of a pewter plate coated in Bitumen of Judea to light within a camera obscura. The areas of the plate that are exposed to light become hardened, and unexposed areas of the plate can be washed away. The plate can then be displayed as a singular photographic image, or it can be used to mechanically print copies of the image using ink.

Lumen print

Similar in process to a cyanotype, a **lumen print** is a contact print exposed in direct sunlight on silver gelatin photographic paper. The result is the silhouette of the photographed object.

Photogenic drawing

Photogenic drawing is a historic term coined by Henry Fox Talbot that refers to a photographic image, particularly a photogram or contact print.

Photogram

A **photogram** is a photographic image produced using light-sensitive paper and development chemicals, but without the use of a camera. The method for producing a photogram typically involves arranging an object or objects on light-sensitive paper before exposing the composition to light, thus capturing the silhouette of the arrangement.

Test strip

Used in traditional darkroom printing, a **test strip** is a series of exposures of different durations of a single image. By developing and evaluating this image, the artist can select the appropriate length of exposure for the final print.

Artist Biographies

Yto Barrada
Moroccan-French, b. 1971

Yto Barrada is a multidisciplinary artist whose work explores themes of borderlands, archival record, and the navigation of life in a political landscape. Her work has been exhibited at the Tate Modern; Museum of Modern Art, New York (MoMA); the Renaissance Society (Chicago); Witte de With (Rotterdam); Haus der Kunst (Munich); Centre Georges Pompidou (Paris); Whitechapel Gallery (London); and the Venice Biennale (2007, 2011). Barrada studied history and political science at the Sorbonne University of Paris and photography at the International Center for Photography in New York City.

Anthea Behm
Australian, b. 1977

Anthea Behm is an artist working in photography, video, and performance. Most recently, her work explores themes of feminism, body, and power in conversation with the work of modern photographers such as Edward Weston and Man Ray. Behm received her MFA from the School of the Art Institute of Chicago. She is Assistant Professor of Photography at the University of Florida, Gainesville, where she lives and works.

Iñaki Bonillas
Mexican, b. 1981

Iñaki Bonillas isolates elements of the photographic act (camera, film, shutter, and darkroom practice) to be reassembled in his work from a new perspective. Bonillas's work has been exhibited across North America and Europe, including the Museum of Modern Art (Mexico City), La Virreina Centre de la Imatge (Barcelona), and the Museum of Modern Art (Paris). He lives and works in Mexico City.

Jillian Marie Browning
American, b. 1989

Jillian Marie Browning (she/they) creates intersectional work exploring feminism and Black identity through multidisciplinary mediums. Browning received her BS in photography from the University of Central Florida and her MFA in studio art from Florida State University. Their work has been acquired by Center for Photography at Woodstock, The Southeast Museum of Photography, and the University of Maryland's David C. Driskell Center for the Study of Visual Arts and Culture of African Americans and the African Diaspora.

Ellen Carey
American, b. 1952

Ellen Carey is an educator, scholar, curator, photographer, and lens-based artist. Her experimental photographic work has been widely exhibited, including at the Amon Carter Museum of American Art (Fort Worth), the Norton Museum of Art (West Palm Beach), and the McCord Museum (Montreal). She published her first artist book, *Mirrors of Chance: The Photograms of Ellen Carey*, in 2017. Carey divides her time between New York and Hartford, Connecticut.

Granville Carroll
American, b. 1992

Granville Carroll is a visual artist, Afrofuturist, and educator whose experimental photographic work explores themes of Blackness, identity, and the universe. Carroll was named a 2022 NYSCA/NYFA Fellow and JGS Photography Fellow, a 2021 Silver List artist, AIR with Visual Studies Workshop (2021), and a 2020 Critical Mass Finalist. He received a BFA from Arizona State University and an MFA from Rochester Institute of Technology.

Danica Chappell
Australian, b. 1972

Danica Chappell makes abstracted photographic work through a darkroom practice. Chappell is the 2020 recipient of the Creative Victoria Sustaining Creative Workers Grant. She received her MFA from Victorian College of the Arts. Chappell lives and works on the traditional lands of the Boon Wurrung and Wurundjeri, in Naarm (Melbourne, Australia).

Elizabeth M. Claffey
American, b. 1980

Elizabeth Claffey is a multimedia artist and photographer whose work explores themes of identity, kinship, the body, and cultural/institutional practice. Claffey was a 2019–20 Research Fellow at the Kinsey Institute for Research in Sex, Gender, and Reproduction and a 2012 William J. Fulbright Fellow. She received her MFA in studio art and a Graduate Certificate in women's studies from Texas Women's University. Claffey is Associate Professor of Photography at Indiana University, Bloomington.

Judith Nangala Crispin
Australian–Bpangerang/Gunaikurnai, b. 1970

Judith Nangala Crispin is a poet and visual artist whose ethereal photographic work makes use of animal bodies and plant matter. Much of her work deals with the cultural history of the Warlpiri people. Crispin is a member of Oculi Collective, a chapter lead of Women Photograph (Sydney), the 2021 Artist in Residence with Music Viva, and the Poetry Editor of *The Canberra Times*. She is based in Canberra, Australia.

Gohar Dashti
Iranian, b. 1980

Gohar Dashti is a photographic artist whose work addresses social issues related to human-geographical narratives, "home" and "displacement," and the natural world. Dashti's work is held by collections around the globe, including the Victoria and Albert Museum (London); Museum of Fine Arts, Boston; Smithsonian National Museum of Asian Art (Washington, DC); and Museum of Contemporary Photography (Chicago). She received her BA and MA in photography from Tehran University of Art. Dashti lives and works in Cambridge, Massachusetts.

Hernease Davis
American, b. 1982

Hernease Davis creates immersive spaces of rest for herself and others through multimedia installations. She has exhibited with Transformer Station (Cleveland), International Center of Photography (NYC), Visual Studies Workshop (Rochester), Tiger Strike Asteroid (Brooklyn), Houston Center for Photography, and Silver Eye Center (Pittsburgh). Davis earned her MFA from ICP-BARD and currently teaches in the MFA program at the Visual Studies Workshop in Rochester, New York.

Marta Djourina
Bulgarian-German, b. 1991

Marta Djourina explores the translation of light from source to carrier through the performative gesture. She has been featured in exhibitions at the Berlinische Galerie, Sofia Arsenal—Museum of Contemporary Art, FeldbuschWiesnerRudolph Galerie (Berlin), and Center d'art Neuchâtel. Currently, she is an Artist-in-Residence at the Federal Foreign Office (Berlin) and a member of Goldrausch Künstlerinnenprojekt. Djourina lives and works in Berlin, Germany.

Chris Duncan
American, b. 1974

Chris Duncan's artworks act as markers of time and a method for capturing sites and objects that are part of his life and practice. His work is in the collections of the Berkeley Art Museum (Berkeley, CA); Kemper Art Museum (St. Louis); MoMA; and San Francisco Museum of Modern Art (SFMoMA), among others. Duncan received his BFA from California College of Arts and Crafts and his MFA from Stanford University. He is currently based in Oakland, California.

Joy Episalla
American, b. 1960

Joy Episalla (she/they) is an interdisciplinary artist whose work repositions photographic and moving image practices into the territory of sculpture, while also engaging queer/feminist perspective. Their work has been collected by the Baltimore Museum of Art, Centre Pompidou, Victoria & Albert Museum (London), and Albright Knox Gallery (Buffalo, NY), among others. Since 1991, Episalla has been a member of fierce pussy art collective.

Julio Grinblatt
Argentinian, b. 1960

Julio Grinblatt is a conceptual artist focused on photography and the logic of taxonomies. His work is represented in collections that include the Museum of Fine Arts Houston; Portland Art Museum (Portland, OR); Samuel P. Harn Museum of Art (Gainesville, FL); Light Work Permanent Collection (Syracuse, NY); Museo Nacional de Bellas Artes and Museo de Arte Moderno de Buenos Aires (both Buenos Aires, Argentina); and Museum of Modern Art (Rio de Janeiro, Brazil). Grinblatt is currently based in Brooklyn, New York.

Sheree Hovsepian
Iranian-American, b. 1974

Sheree Hovsepian is a New York–based artist who explores the performative and bodily functions of line and shape through photography, drawing, and collage. Hovsepian's work is in the collections of the Guggenheim Museum, Bronx Museum of the Arts, Art Institute of Chicago, Studio Museum (Harlem, NY), and Everson Museum at Syracuse University. Hovsepian earned a BFA/BA from University of Toledo and an MFA from the School of the Art Institute of Chicago.

Roberto Huarcaya
Peruvian, b. 1959

Roberto Huarcaya employs cameraless techniques as a way to capture the complexities of the changing natural world. His work is held in the collections of the Maison Européenne de la Photographie (Paris); Museum of Fine Arts, Houston; Fototeca Latinoamericana (Buenos Aires); and Museo Universitario de Arte Contemporáneo, Mexico City, among others. He holds a degree in psychology from the Universidad Católica del Perú, Lima, and studied cinema at the Instituto Italiano (Lima) and photography at Centro del Video y la Imagen (Madrid).

Nikolai Ishchuk
British-Russian, b. 1982

Nikolai Ishchuk works with experimental photo-based, mixed-media, and sculptural processes. His work has been exhibited internationally at institutions such as Whitechapel Gallery, Moscow Museum of Art, K11 (Shanghai), and Fotomuseum Winterthur. Ishchuk earned an M.Phil in modern society and global transformations from University of Cambridge and an MA in fine art from the Chelsea College of Art in London, where he currently lives and works.

Kei Ito
Japanese, b. 1991

Kei Ito's work addresses intergenerational connection and loss through experimental processes. He has been an Artist in Residence at MASS MoCA, Center for Fine Art Photography, and Creative Alliance, among others. Ito's work is included in public collections such as the Museum of Contemporary Photography (Chicago), Norton Museum of Art (West Palm Beach), and California Institute of Integral Arts. He earned his MFA from Maryland Institute College of Art and his BFA from Rochester Institute of Technology.

Priya Suresh Kambli
Indian-American, b. 1975

Priya Suresh Kambli is a photographic artist who examines the formation and erasure of identity as part of the migrant experience. Kambli's work has been collected by the Archive of Documentary Arts Collection at Duke University; Museum of Fine Arts, Houston; and Museum of Contemporary Photography (Chicago). She received her BFA at the University of Louisiana in Lafayette and an MFA from the University of Houston. Kambli is currently Professor of Art at Truman State University in Kirksville, Missouri.

Laurie Kang
Korean-Canadian, b. 1985

Laurie Kang has exhibited at the New Museum, SculptureCenter, and Cue Art Foundation (all New York); The Power Plant (Toronto); and Camera Austria (Graz). She was the inaugural artist-in-residence at Horizon Art Foundation (Los Angeles) in 2022 and has completed additional artist residencies in Banff, Alberta; Vilnius, Lithuania; and Bergen, Norway. Kang holds an MFA from the Milton Avery School of the Arts at Bard College. She lives and works in Toronto, Canada.

Farrah Karapetian
American, b. 1978

Farrah Karapetian works with photography phenomenologically to mine memory and reveal agency. Her artwork is in public collections that include the J. Paul Getty Museum, the Los Angeles County Museum of Art, and SFMoMA. Karapetian has been an Art Prospect Network Fellow in Tashkent, Uzbekistan; COLA Individual Artist Fellow; and Fulbright Scholar. She holds an MFA from the University of California at Los Angeles and a BA from Yale University. Karapetian is currently Assistant Professor of Photography at the University of San Diego.

Tatiana Kronberg

American,
b. Ukraine, 1979

Tatiana Kronberg employs photograms, performance, and sculpture—often together—in pursuit of images as active events. Her work has been exhibited at the International Center of Photograph (New York); Torrance Art Museum (Los Angeles); and Artists' Space (New York). Kronberg holds an MFA from Bard+ICP in advanced photographic studies.

Galina Kurlat

Russian Jewish-
American, b. 1981

Galina Kurlat creates a visual relationship between herself and her subject by embracing the imperfections and possibilities of antiquated photographic processes. Her work has been exhibited in Finland, South Korea, India, Scotland, France, and the United States. Kurlat's work is held in a number of public and private collections, including the Museum of Fine Arts Houston and the Harry Ransom Center (Austin). She lives and works in Brooklyn, New York.

David Ondrik

American, b. 1976

David Ondrik works primarily with analogue film processes, alternative printing techniques, and abstraction to examine photography's capacity for memory and reflection. His artwork is held by the New Mexico Museum of Art, the University of New Mexico Art Museum, New Mexico public art collections, and the Indiana University Health Bloomington Hospital. He holds a BFA in studio art from the University of New Mexico and an MFA in studio art from Indiana University, where he is a Lecturer in Photography.

Dakota Mace

Diné, b. 1991

Dakota Mace is a Diné (Navajo) interdisciplinary artist whose work focuses on translating the language of Diné history and beliefs. Mace's work is in collections such as MoMA; Smithsonian National Museum of the American Indian (Washington, DC); and Institute of American Indian Arts (Santa Fe). She received her MA and MFA degrees in photography and textile design at the University of Wisconsin-Madison and her BFA in photography from the Institute of American Indian Arts.

Amanda Marchand

Canadian, b. 1968

Amanda Marchand explores the natural world through experimental photographic processes. Most recently, her work has been exhibited at Institute of Contemporary Art at MECA (ME), Turner Contemporary (UK), Datz Museum (Korea), Center for Contemporary Arts (NM), the Center for Fine Art Photography (CO), the Palo Alto Art Center (CA), and Traywick Contemporary (CA). Marchand received her MFA from the San Francisco Art Institute and currently lives and works in Brooklyn, NY.

Aspen Mays

American, b. 1980

Aspen Mays looks to everyday objects and archival materials to inform her darkroom practice. She has had solo exhibitions at the Museum of Contemporary Art (Chicago) and Light Work (Syracuse, NY), and was included in the Crystal Bridges Museum of American Art's national survey of American contemporary art. Mays has been the recipient of a Fulbright Scholarship and Rotary Fellowship. She earned her BA from the University of North Carolina, Chapel Hill and her MFA from the School of the Art Institute of Chicago. Mays currently serves as Associate Professor and Chair of Undergraduate Photography at California College of the Arts in San Francisco.

Brent Meistre

South African,
b. 1975

Brent Meistre is an artist, curator, and filmmaker, whose serial photographic, stop-motion, and film work explore sites and objects related to post-conflict and post-Cold War Africa. Meistre also co-founded Analogue Eye, a mobile curatorial platform that focuses on artists from, or working in, Africa. He earned a Post Graduate Diploma in higher education and an MFA, both with distinction, from Rhodes University. Meistre lives and works in Belfast, Northern Ireland.

Fabiola Menchelli
Mexican, b. 1983

Fabiola Menchelli's work investigates essential ideas about photography through the language of abstraction and poetry. She has held residencies at Skowhegan School of Painting and Sculpture and Bemis Center for Contemporary Arts, and received awards from the Mexican Photography Biennial of the Centra de la Imagen and National System of Art Creators (National Fund for Culture and the Arts, Mexico). Menchelli holds an MFA in photography and visual arts from Massachusetts College of Art and Design and a BFA in computer-mediated arts. She lives and works in Mexico City.

Osamu James Nakagawa
Japanese-American, b. 1962

Osamu James Nakagawa's work explores the landscape of the Japanese prefecture Okinawa and US-Japan relations. Nakagawa was the recipient of a Guggenheim Fellowship, and previously named Higashikawa New Photographer of the Year and Sagamihara Photographer of the Year. His work has been exhibited at the Tokyo Photographic Art Museum, the Kunstmuseum Brandts (Odense), and the Metropolitan Museum of Art, among others. Nakagawa received a BA from the University of St. Thomas Houston and an MFA in photography from the University of Houston. Currently, he is the Ruth N. Halls Distinguished Professor of Photography at Indiana University.

Nadezda Nikolova
Croatian-Bulgarian-American, b. 1978

Born in former Yugoslavia/present-day Serbia, Nadezda Nikolova studied nineteenth-century phototrophic printing processes at the University of Kentucky and the George Eastman Museum. Nikolova's work has been exhibited at the Center for Photographic Art (Carmel, CA), California Museum of Photography, and Photo London. She holds a BA in environmental science and MA in policy analysis. She is based in Oakland, California.

Lisa Oppenheim
American, b. 1975

Lisa Oppenheim creates photographs and videos that connect historical imagery and techniques with the present through research-based practice. She received her BA from Brown University and an MFA from the Milton Avery Graduate School for the Arts at Bard College. She also participated in the Whitney Independent Study Program and Rijksakademie van beeldedne kunsten in Amsterdam. Oppenheim lives and works in New York City.

Letícia Ramos
Brazilian, b. 1976

Letícia Ramos explores the limits of the production and exegesis of analog images through photographic and filmic works, which she also develops into installations, objects, publications, and performances. She addresses aesthetic intersections between the documentary and the fictional, occurring between natural and imaginary landscapes and discourses of historical records and invented characters. Ramos's selected solo exhibitions include the Jeu de Paume (Paris), Fundación Botín (Santander), and Pivô (São Paulo). She lives and works in São Paulo, Brazil.

Mariah Robertson
American, b. 1975

Mariah Robertson investigates themes of representation and reproduction through rigorous darkroom experimentation. Robertson's work has been exhibited in solo and group exhibitions at BALTIC Centre for Contemporary Art (UK); Grand Arts (Kansas City); Contemporary Arts Museum, Houston; and Cleveland Museum of Art's Transformer Station. Her work is in the collections of the Whitney Museum of American Art; MoMA; and LACMA, among others. Robertson received her BA from University of California, Berkeley, and her MFA from Yale University. She lives and works in Brooklyn, New York.

Anna Katharina Scheidegger
Swiss, b. 1976

Anna Katharina Scheidegger works between photography, performance, and video. Her photographs are held by the National Fund of Contemporary Arts of France, the collection Société Général, Ing Real Estate Photography Collection, and the Maison Européenne de la Photographie, Paris. Scheidegger graduated with distinction from the École nationale supérieure des Arts Décoratifs Paris in 2003 and Le Fresnoy—Studio national des arts contemporains. Scheidegger lives and works in Paris, France, and Bern, Switzerland.

Stefanie Seufert
German, b. 1969

Stefanie Seufert explores the relationship between visibility, language, and architecture through primarily cameraless processes. Her work has been exhibited at Berlinische Galerie, Kunsthalle Darmstadt, NRW-Forum Düsseldorf, Museum für Fotografie (Berlin), Camera Austria (Graz), and Kasbah Museum (Tangier), among others. Seufert's work is in the collections of Berlinische Galerie, DZ Bank Frankfurt, NBK Berlin, Kunstbibliothek, Staatliche Museen zu Berlin, and various private collections. She holds degrees in photography from Lette Verein Berlin and cultural studies from Universität der Künste, Berlin, where she also lives and works.

Assaf Shaham
Israeli, b. 1983

Assaf Shaham uses sculpture, video, photography, and installation to provoke reflections on established systems and power structures that underlie social and economic issues. Shaham's work has been exhibited at institutions that include the Herzliya Museum of Contemporary Art, Tel Aviv Museum of Art, and Santa Barbara Center for Art. He earned a BFA from the Minshar School of Art and an MFA from the University of Southern California. Shaham divides his time between Tel Aviv, Israel, and Los Angeles, California.

David Benjamin Sherry
American, b. 1981

David Benjamin Sherry addresses environmentalism, queer identity, and abstraction through alternative analogue film processes. Sherry's work is held in the permanent collections of the Alfond Collection of Contemporary Art, Cornell Fine Arts Museum, Charles Saatchi Collection (London), Hood Museum of Art, LACMA, Marciano Art Foundation, the Nasher Museum of Art, RISD Museum, Walker Art Center, Wexner Center for the Arts, and the Whitney Museum of American Art. He received a BFA from Rhode Island School of Design and his MFA from Yale University. Sherry currently lives and works in Santa Fe, New Mexico.

Iswanto Soerjanto
Indonesian, b. 1967

Iswanto Soerjanto's practice joins alternative processes, including chemigrams and cyanotypes, with philosophies rooted in Eastern culture. Originally trained as an advertising photographer, he sought to move beyond the traditional boundaries of the digital camera to instead experiment with camera obscura, tintypes, and glass plates. Soerjanto's work has been shown in institutions across Indonesia, Singapore, and Western Europe. He currently lives and works in Jakarta, Indonesia.

Justine Varga
Australian, b. 1984

Justine Varga explores the conceptual possibilities of photography through sustained interrogation of its chemical, material, and conceptual properties. She was the recipient of the Josephine Ulrick and Win Shubert Foundation for the Arts Photography Award (2013, 2016), Olive Cotton Award for Photographic Portraiture (2017), and Dobell Drawing Prize (2019). Her work was recently published in *Installation View: Photography Exhibitions in Australia 1848–2020* and *Negative/ Positive: A History of Photography* (both 2021).

Daisuke Yokota
Japanese, b. 1983

Daisuke Yokota focuses on photographic temporality and materiality by engaging in destructive processing techniques. Yokota's work has been exhibited at Foam (Amsterdam); Museum of Fine Arts, Boston; and Rencontres d'Arles. He is the recipient of the Foam Paul Huf Award and Photo London John Kobal Residency Award. Yokota's work is held in numerous collections, including SFMoMA; MFA Boston; and Fotomuseum Winterthur. He earned his advanced degree at Nippon Photography Institute in Tokyo, Japan.

Selected Bibliography

Anderson, Christina Z. *Cyanotype: The Blueprint in Contemporary Practice*. Contemporary Practices in Alternative Process Photography Series. London: Routledge, Taylor and Francis Group, 2019.

Anderson, Dave, and Will Steacy, eds. *Photographs Not Taken: A Collection of Photographer's Essays*. Hillsborough: Daylight Community Arts Foundation, 2012.

Arnhold, Hermann, Kristin Bartels, Ulrike Gärtner, Torsten Blume, Tanja Pirsig-Marshall, Julie Jones, and Eline van Dijk, eds. *Bauhaus and America: Experiments in Light and Movement*. 1st ed. Bielefeld: Kerber Art, 2018. Exhibition catalog.

Arnold, Brian. *Alternate Processes in Photography: Technique, History, and Creative Potential*. New York: Oxford University Press, 2017.

Arnow, Jan. *Handbook of Alternative Photographic Processes*. New York: Van Nostrand Reinhold, 1982.

Atkins, Anna, and Rolf Sachsse. *Anna Atkins—Blue Prints*. Edited by Marion Blomeyer. Munich: Hirmer, 2021.

Atkins, Anna, Larry J. Schaaf, and Hans P. Kraus. *Sun Gardens: Victorian Photograms*. New York: Aperture, 1985.

Azoulay, Ariella. "Photography—The Ontological Question." *Mafte/akh* 2e (2011): 65–80.

Barnes, Martin. *Shadow Catchers, Camera-Less Photography*. 2nd ed. London: Victoria and Albert Museum; London: Merrell Publishers, 2012. Exhibition catalog.

_____. *Cameraless Photography*. London: Victoria and Albert Museum; London: Thames & Hudson, 2019. Exhibition catalog.

Baker, Simon, Emmanuelle de L'Ecotais, and Shoair Mavlian, eds. *Shape of Light: 100 Years of Photography and Abstract Art*. London: Tate; New York: D.A.P, 2018. Exhibition catalog.

Barnier, John, ed. *Coming into Focus: A Step-by-Step Guide to Alternative Photographic Printing Processes*. San Francisco: Chronicle Books, 2000.

Batchen, Geoffrey. *Emanations: The Art of the Cameraless Photograph*. New York: DelMonico Books; Munich: Prestel, 2016. Exhibition catalog.

Bossen, Howard. *Henry Holmes Smith: Man of Light*. Studies in Photography. 1st ed. Ann Arbor, MI: UMI Research Press, 1983.

Cotton, Charlotte. *The Photograph as Contemporary Art*. 2nd ed. Thames & Hudson World of Art. London: Thames & Hudson, 2009.

Engelbrecht, Lloyd C. "Educating the Eye: Photography and the Founding Generation at the Institute of Design, 1937–1946." In *Taken by Design: Photographs from the Institute of Design, 1937–1971*, edited by David Travis and Elizabeth Siegel, 16–33. Chicago: Art Institute of Chicago; Chicago: University of Chicago Press, 2002. Exhibition catalog.

Fried, Michael. *Why Photography Matters as Art as Never Before*. New Haven, Yale University Press, 2008.

Grundberg, Andy. *How Photography Became Contemporary Art: Inside an Artistic Revolution from Pop to the Digital Age*. New Haven: Yale University Press, 2021.

Haffer, Virna. *Making Photograms: The Creative Process of Painting with Light*. Visual Communication Books. New York: Hastings House, 1969.

Hahn, Betty. "Henry Holmes Smith: Speaking with a Genuine Voice." *Image* 16, no. 4 (December 1973): 3.

Heckert, Virginia, Marc Harnly, and Sarah Freeman. *Light, Paper, Process: Reinventing Photography*. Los Angeles: J. Paul Getty Museum, 2015. Exhibition catalog.

Hershberger, Andrew E., ed. *Photographic Theory: An Historical Anthology*. Chichester: Wiley Blackwell, 2014.

Holter, Patra. *Photography without a Camera*. New York: Nostrand Reinhold, 1972.

James, Christopher. *The Book of Alternative Photographic Processes*. 2nd ed. Clifton Park, NY: Delmar Cengage Learning, 2009.

Kenaan, Hagi. *Photography and Its Shadow*. Stanford, CA: Stanford University Press, 2020.

Kennel, Sarah, Diane Waggoner, and Alice Carver-Kubik, eds. *In the Darkroom: An Illustrated Guide to Photographic Processes Before the Digital Age*. Washington, DC: Thames & Hudson, 2010.

Klein, Alex, Charlotte Cotton, and Los Angeles County Museum of Art, eds. *Words without Pictures*. 1st ed. New York: Aperture, 2009.

Livingstone, Margaret S. *Vision and Art (Updated and Expanded Edition): The Biology of Seeing*. New York: Abrams, 2013.

Lloyd, Jill, and Michael Peppiatt. *Christian Schad and the Neue Sachlichkeit*. New York: Neue Galerie New York; New York: W. W. Norton, 2003. Exhibition catalog.

McDonald, Jessica S. "Introducing 'The Niépce Heliograph.'" *Harry Ransom Center Magazine*, University of Texas, Austin. Last modified August 20, 2019. https://sites.utexas.edu/ransomcentermagazine/2019/08/20/introducing-the-niepce-heliograph/.

Moholy-Nagy, László. *The New Vision: Fundamentals of Bauhaus Design, Painting, Sculpture, and Architecture*. 4th ed. New York: Wittenborn, Schultz, 1949.

Morris-Reich, Amos, and Margaret Rose Olin, eds. *Photography and Imagination*. Routledge History of Photography. New York: Routledge, Taylor & Francis Group, 2020.

Neusüss, Floris Michael, Thomas F. Barrow, and Charles Hagen, eds. *Experimental Vision: The Evolution of the Photogram since 1919*. Niwot, CO: Denver Art Museum; New York: Roberts Rinehart Publishers, 1994.

Rexer, Lyle. *Photography's Antiquarian Avant-Garde: The New Wave in Old Processes*. New York: Harry N. Abrams, 2002.

_____. *The Edge of Vision: The Rise of Abstraction in Photography*. 1st ed. New York: Aperture, 2009.

Rohrbach, John, and Sylvie Pénichon, eds. *Color: American Photography Transformed*. 1st ed. Austin: Amon Carter Museum of American Art; Austin: University of Texas Press, 2013. Exhibition catalog.

Rubinstein, Daniel, ed. *Fragmentation of the Photographic Image in the Digital Age*. Routledge History of Photography. New York: Routledge, Taylor & Francis Group, 2020.

Schaaf, Larry J, ed. *Sun Gardens: Cyanotypes by Anna Atkins*. New York: Prestel, 2018.

Schwarz, Maureen Trudelle. *Fighting Colonialism with Hegemonic Culture: Native American Appropriation of Indian Stereotypes*. Albany, NY: SUNY Press, 2013.

Squiers, Carol, Geoffrey Batchen, George Baker, and Hito Steyerl, eds. *What Is a Photograph?* New York: International Center of Photography; New York: DelMonico Books-Prestel, 2013. Exhibition catalog.

Statzer, Mary, ed. *The Photographic Object 1970*. Oakland: University of California Press, 2016.

Tishman, Shari. *Slow Looking: The Art and Practice of Learning Through Observation*. New York: Routledge, Taylor & Francis Group, 2018.

Webb, Randall, and Martin Reed. *Alternative Photographic Processes: A Working Guide for Image Makers*. Rochester, NY: Silver Pixel Press, 2000.

Weinberger, Norman S. *Art of the Photogram: Photography without a Camera*. New York: Taplinger Publishing, 1981.

Wilks, Brady. *Alternative Photographic Processes: Crafting Handmade Images*. New York: Focal Press, Taylor & Francis Group, 2015.

About the Author

Lauren Richman is Assistant Curator of Photography at the Sidney and Lois Eskenazi Museum of Art at Indiana University, Bloomington, where she oversees the Henry Holmes Smith Archive. Prior to joining the staff of the Eskenazi Museum, she held curatorial and research roles at the Smithsonian American Art Museum, Amon Carter Museum of American Art, Art Institute of Chicago, and New Orleans Museum of Art. Richman's research has been supported by the Henry Luce Foundation, Smithsonian American Art Museum, Terra Foundation for American Art, and Dallas Museum of Art. She holds a PhD and MA in art history from Southern Methodist University, and BA in the same subject from Vanderbilt University.